TO
LIVE
IN
LOVE

Also by Eileen Guder

What Happened After ... Ten Plays based on
New Testament incidents

We're Never Alone
A modern woman looks at her world

TO
LIVE
IN
LOVE

Eileen Guder

Foreword by
Helmut Thielicke

Introduction by
Richard C. Halverson

Zondervan Publishing House
Grand Rapids, Michigan

TO
LIVE
IN
LOVE

For Darrell, Donna, Linda, Michael
with love

FOREWORD

To Live in Love is a study of the thirteenth chapter of
I Corinthians, a text which is almost too well known. Mrs.
Guder, however, succeeds in taking us on a vivid, serious
and promising adventure in the overused word, "love." She
lets Paul speak directly to our bright or gray daily life
— concretely, practically, undogmatically.

The book overflows with reality. It speaks of our fears
and loneliness, our marital problems, the rearing of our
children, the humor of love. It tells stories and describes
people. And it provides specific directions and aids for life,
yet without any legalism.

The complaint has often been expressed that Protestant
churches give their members so little spiritual leadership and
help. Here, now, is a book full of concrete, spiritual wisdom.

HELMUT THIELICKE, D.D.
University of Hamburg, Germany

INTRODUCTION

Here is a penetrating, practical, personal commentary on the classic chapter on love, I Corinthians 13. With a distinctive, drawn-from-life analysis, the love about which Paul wrote is seen in its day-to-day relevance to the commonplace. Diagnosing as she goes, the author never fails to apply the remedy in each chapter.

Eileen Guder writes as she lives — down to earth. She is no stranger to the academic, but the strength of this book is in its clinical insights. As daughter, woman, wife, mother and friend, she has come by this understanding the hard way — through the valley of the shadow, by the way of tragedy, the wounded way of shattered hopes and devastating disappointments. She speaks out of the triumph Christ gives through the agonizing, lingering illnesses and deaths of a lovely daughter and, very recently, a beloved husband. Authenticity comes through page after page.

Eileen never just accepted anything, least of all herself, easily. She is not incredulous, but constitutionally she has to be "shown." She is delightfully convincing when simple demonstration is forthcoming, and *To Live in Love* reflects this practical, empirical approach to life which is her hallmark.

This book probably does not contain anything you do not know already, but it will remind you often — and with surgical efficiency — of things you have deliberately ignored, or conveniently forgotten. It may not "tease" the intellect, but it will blast inactivity and apathy.

If you want to continue living a stereotyped, conventional, innocuous "Christian" life, it will be a mistake to read this book. But if you want to be a real person, as was our incarnate Lord, this will be just "what the doctor ordered."

Eileen Guder has put the "how" in this book — not just a static criterion against which to measure or toward which to strive, but the "how" of fulfillment.

This book won't change the world perhaps, but it will help to change those in the world who read it.

RICHARD C. HALVERSON
Minister, Fourth Presbyterian Church, Washington, D.C.

ANOTHER BOOK ON LOVE?

Some sort of disclaimer seems called for when the title of a book contains the word, "Love." Readers tend to expect one of two approaches: (a) love in its romantic, or sexual aspect; or (b) a complicated and technical theological dissertation.

If the first approach is used one can be sure of all sorts of highly interesting chapters on such subjects as the necessity of keeping romance alive, and so forth. Both the readers not yet married and those long since settled into marriage may find large gaps between the parts that seem to apply to *their* situation. If the theological view of love is the basis of the book there will be some careful analysis of the three Greek words used to express love; and some nice distinctions between brotherly love, the grace of God, and romantic love.

All this is very necessary and certainly helpful. Yet there is still more to be said. What is the use of knowing whether Paul used the Greek word for brotherly love or sexual love if, whichever variety we happen to be coping with at the moment, we are making a botch of it? This book is written from a still different viewpoint: for, whatever Greek the Bible uses when it speaks of love, the Scriptures are mainly concerned with how love behaves.

For this reason, all the Bible passages about love that are referred to in the book are gathered together in a "Glossary of Love" starting on page 187. There are others in the Bible, of course, but they generally reiterate what is said in the ones I have chosen.

To be sure, what I've written is partial and imperfect,

for I am just an imperfect human being, seeing and understanding only fragmentarily. But the Bible gives us this positive assertion — our love is to have a certain stamp upon it, whether for parent or child or friend or lover; and that identifying mark is seen in our words and actions and attitudes. By such means we communicate or interpret ourselves to others. In this sense — *love is what you do.*

CONTENTS

Foreword by Helmut Thielicke

Introduction by Richard C. Halverson

Another Book on Love?

1   The Magic Key 17

2   Love in Action 35

3   Love Without Greed 51

4   Rx Humor 69

5   Always in Style 83

6   Doin' What Comes Naturally 99

7   ". . . To Forget, Divine" 110

8   Yesterday, Today, Forever 128

9   Danger —
    Approach with Caution 144

10 Grow Up! 154

11 God's Secrets 169

12 We Do What We Are 178

Glossary of Love 187

TO
LIVE
IN
LOVE

I CORINTHIANS 13

If I speak with the eloquence of men and of angels, but have no love, I become no more than blaring brass or crashing cymbal. If I have the gift of fortelling the future and hold in my mind not only all human knowledge but the very secrets of God, and if I also have that absolute faith which can move mountains, but have no love, I amount to nothing at all. If I dispose of all that I possess, yes, even if I give my own body to be burned, but have no love, I achieve precisely nothing.

This love of which I speak is slow to lose patience — it looks for a way of being constructive. It is not possessive: it is neither anxious to impress nor does it cherish inflated ideas of its own importance.

Love has good manners and does not pursue selfish advantage. It is not touchy. It does not keep account of evil or gloat over the wickedness of other people. On the contrary, it is glad with all good men when truth prevails.

Love knows no limit to its endurance, no end to its trust, no fading of its hope; it can outlast anything. It is, in fact, the one thing that still stands when all else has fallen.

For if there are prophecies they will be fulfilled and done with, if there are "tongues" the need for them will disappear, if there is knowledge it will be swallowed up in truth. For our knowledge is always incomplete and our prophecy is always incomplete, and when the complete comes, that is the end of the incomplete.

When I was a little child I talked and felt and thought like a little child. Now that I am a man my childish speech and feeling and thought have no further significance for me.

At present we are men looking at puzzling reflections in a mirror. The time will come when we shall see reality whole and face to face! At present all I know is a little fraction of the truth, but the time will come when I shall know it as fully as God now knows me!

In this life we have three great lasting qualities — faith, hope and love. But the greatest of them is love.

(From *The New Testament in Modern English*
Translated by J. B. Phillips)

1. THE
MAGIC
KEY

*You should set your hearts on the best spiritual gifts, but I
shall show you a way which surpasses them all.*

— I Corinthians 12:31

Love is not enough!

What a shocking thing to say, yet it is true. The warm
tide of shapeless sentimentality commonly called "love" works
as much harm as good in the world. Jealous rages, callous
selfishness, and the most blatant falsity are all excused on
the grounds of love. Either love is no unmixed blessing or
our idea of it has gone wrong.

Frankly, I think the latter is the case. Love in the New
Testament is never sentimentalized or recommended without definition. It is always described *in action*, so *we can
see what it is by what it does.*

In spite of all the sloppy thinking about love, we know
that it — or something vaguely like it — is desperately needed. In a world full of contradictions and cross purposes

there are not too many things just about everyone agrees on. Christians and non-Christians alike, whatever our differences on most things, do agree that there ought to be more love in the world. Love is the magic key of life.

Yes, love is the magic key of life — not to get what we want, but to become what we ought to be. All of us want this magic key, but sometimes we try to unlock the wrong doors with it. This book is about the key — and the right doors.

Substitutions For Love

We can easily see why the non-Christian world, separated from God and lost in self-seeking should be unable to find love, or, having found it, to keep it. Everyone tends to look for love *from* others, to fill the need in his life. "Love me and I will love you in return." Sometimes it works that way — for those who are gifted, beautiful or brilliant. More often such a blind search for love ends in futility, a desperate game of blind-man's-bluff played by men and women blundering about. Each one has his own little bucket, empty and waiting to be filled with love, but with no love of his own to pour out for someone else.

For all who have come to know Christ, however, the picture has changed. God loves us. He has poured out His love upon us, not with a careful and measured hand, but with incomprehensible generosity, splashing and overflowing our tiny containers. Enough so that we can channel that amazing love out to thirsty people.

How? I remember when I first became a Christian thinking, "Now I must love everyone. But how shall I love them, they provoke me so? (They are still as irritating and difficult as ever.) I know — I'll witness to them! They certainly need the love of Christ." Behind my thinking lay the unexpressed thought that it would be impossible to really love people until they "shaped up." So instead of realizing that loving was witnessing, I thought that witnessing was loving. Yet according to the New Testament we are not called on to present a manifesto from God, or to explain a new set of rules, but to show what He has done for us. "Look," we can cry to the world, "my bucket is full! God loves me, see what He's done for me. And there's more, for everyone — all you can hold! Come and see how wonderful it is!"

But why don't they hear? What shall we do to get them to listen to us?

According to Jesus there is a way. "This is how all men will know that you are my disciples, *because you have such love for one another*" (John 13:35, italics added).

No amount of pious prattle, nor tracts handed out, no earnest little homilies delivered to our sceptical friends will convince them of the truth of the Gospel unless they see it in our lives. However loving we may feel toward God, if there is no evidence of love towards others in our attitudes, no one will believe we love God — or have been loved by Him. They can't see our love for God. They *can* see how we behave toward our families and friends, how we react toward people who are irritating or inconvenient. And by our behavior they judge the truth of our love toward God.

As important as our witness is, however, most of us do not want to be more loving for that reason. We feel, in some dim and formless way, that we *ought* to be more loving. The excuses we make for ourselves — "I was tired," "I'd been rushing all day when *this* happened," "He *knew* how late I was already" — only satisfy that shallow level of our thinking we keep on top of our minds for our daily routine. Underneath we are uneasily conscious that it just won't do. Then there are those dreadful times when the husband we sent off to work on the heels of a quarrel, or the child we'd snapped at and told sharply to "for heaven's sake go outside, you're driving me crazy," is late — and the deep wells of our love and anxiety overwhelm us. Why can't we *be* loving when we have so much love within us?

Perhaps the problem is that we are *not* really convinced that love is terribly important. Could it be that in the evangelical Christian world we have substituted piety or piousness (*my* faith, *my* witnessing, *my* devotional life) for love? Do we really take Paul seriously, in the opening words of I Corinthians 13, or do we write him off as overly excited, and the figures of speech as mere poetic exaggerations?

> If I speak with the eloquence of men and of angels, but have no love, I become no more than blaring brass or crashing cymbal. If I have the gift of foretelling the future and hold in my mind not only all human knowledge but the very secrets of God, and if I also have that absolute faith which can move mountains, but have no love, I amount to nothing at all. If I dispose of all that I possess, yes, even if I give my own body to be burned, but have no love, I achieve precisely nothing.

Every age in history has its own climate, and there have been times when Paul's words were neglected. Men have valued other things more than love: duty, honor, the glory of conquest, many things have come first. Other days they needed to hear those words. Our day, on the contrary, seems to be inundated with talk of love. Yet we neglect love too.

But we do talk. And not just about the pagan concept of love as sex, prevalent as that is, but about love that does good and not evil in the world. Rebellious students talk about love, condemning the world of tradition and social forms and patterns of living for its lack of love. Every crusading group out to upset the patterns of life does it on the basis of love — a love they say is lacking in the social order of the day. The Christian world reads and talks and preaches about love.

Since there is such universal agreement on the desirability of love, you'd think there would be more of it in evidence, especially in the Christian world.

Why do we fail?

How do we fail?

The obvious reasons for our ineffectiveness leap to our minds. We are, after all, innately sinful, with a disposition toward selfishness, so that while we want to be loved we find our ability to love hampered by our self-absorption. Our bad habits of thinking acquired over a lifetime are hard to break. Emotional problems make it difficult for us to show the love we feel.

We have seen how easy it is to draw false conclusions by scrambling our definitions — "loving Christian will witness for Christ: I am witnessing; therefore I am loving." Or "loving Christian will read his Bible and pray: I read and pray; therefore I am loving." How hard it is for us to do the obvious or to face the obvious — which is that love itself is the hallmark of the Christian life.

The Church has always tended, because of this horror of the obvious, to substitute other things for love. One branch of the Church has substituted an elaborate system of ritual and legalism for love. Another has made social action so synonymous with Christian love that personal responsibility has become lost in corporate action — the Kingdom is to be brought in by a committee, one assumes.

Most dangerous of all, a large part of the Christian world has replaced love as the center of life with personal piety. Endless talks, books and discussions on one's prayer life or devotions are the staple diet of these people. The burning issue is "How to be spiritual," rather than the practical New Testament emphasis on Christian behavior. Love turns our eyes outward — to others. Personal piety is all inward — how is my prayer life, how pious do I feel, am I really more spiritual this month than last? One can be absorbed in one's own piety and be utterly without love. Is this our condition?

Do we refuse to admit our lovelessness? We hear a great many people say, "I need more faith," but very seldom does one admit, "I am not a loving person. I don't care too much about pleasing God — or anyone else." Perhaps the lack of love from others is so keenly felt, the hurt so sharp that we cannot bear to admit that we, too, are guilty of inflicting such pain by our own unloving attitudes. For then we would be admitting not only a need but a guilt. So to excuse our own failure we point to the shortcomings of others toward us. Yet even so we cannot entirely drown that persistent voice, though we wish we could. No, still we hear the words, "*I* am not loving enough."

Analysis and Commitment

There comes a time in every serious pursuit of truth when we must stop analyzing our predicament and turn to the Bible. George Macdonald said, "Analysis is well, as death is well." No amount of tearing apart, examining, measuring and analyzing can give life. Dead bodies are dissected and studied, but that does not make them live again. "To dissect is to kill," Wordsworth said. So it is with our study of love — or the lack of love — in our lives. When we have finished tearing ourselves apart to see what's wrong, we come up with a diagnosis of the disease. But we must look another place for the cure.

The Bible does not waste many words on analysis but simply states what is wrong. Just as simply it states what we must do. The fact is that our contemporary obsession with self-analysis leads us into the depths of our own helpless selves until we become lost in our own inner workings.

As people used to talk endlessly about their operations, or their digestive problems, now we chatter on about our complexes and traumas. This gets us nowhere.

The Bible tells us to follow a different procedure entirely. We are given guidelines and told to obey them. The men and women who lived in the first days of the growing Church were very much like us. Yet the New Testament tells — commands — the Church to love. If we are commanded to be loving, it is quite probable that God will not be impressed with our excuses — a sobering thought. We are not even allowed to wait until we understand the guidelines. The promise of understanding is contingent upon our obedience.

"If anyone *wants to do* God's will," Jesus told His followers, "he will *know* whether my teaching is from God or whether I merely speak on my own authority" (John 7:17 italics added).

It looks very much as though we are being told that only by *doing* will we know the reasons; that obedience to the law precedes understanding of the law; behaving as if we love precedes enjoying the emotion of love; commitment first, then the reward of knowing. Shocking! It seems to be exactly the opposite of everything we've learned in life. (Yet this is what the scientist does when, already committed to his hypothesis, he takes each verifying step.) First we try to understand, to reason out, the logic of a subject. Then, on the basis of that understanding, we proceed to act on the principle.

We see this on all levels of living. Even children learn very early to demand reasons for their parents' commands — and some schools of psychology would have the parents give a painstaking explanation for everything to the child. It seems logical and right that all of life should be ordered this way. We are thinking beings and must know why we

do what we do. Something must be wrong with the Bible, then, when it tells us first to *do* and then to *know*.

A dislike of any kind of commitment without prior comprehension of reasonableness is one of the hallmarks of our
day. On every level, at every age, it is the dominant note
in our voices. I have heard it so many times, that at a
certain point in a confidence I expect it — the words, "I
just don't know what love is," from young men and women.

We used to think of collegians as impetuous and en-
thusiastic, running headlong into love, so much so that their
elders tried to restrain them. Not any more. Today they
hesitate and analyze. And examine their own feelings until they are paralyzed into immobility. They view the world
about them with the same caution. Not for them the
careless giving of themselves in patriotic fervor — they are
much more likely to embark on a discussion of the morality
of the social order. The comparatively few young people
who have involved themselves in social protest movements
are in sharp contrast to the many who remain untouched
and sceptical about anything that would be "overboard,"
who survey the future coolly, unwilling to lose themselves in
any venture — especially the venture of personal relationships. "Show me why," they say, "and then I'll consider it."

And even the most fervent members of social protest
movements seem to be unwilling to commit themselves to
involvement in a personal relationship. They are involved
in a cause, yes, but along with that cause goes a casual
attitude toward human relationships that eliminates any
responsibility. "Play it cool" is the watchword. When they
talk about "Love," they mean sex — with whomever happens
to be handy and attractive at the moment. No permanent
relationship is considered. Is their headlong plunge into a
"movement" a substitute for any kind of personal involvement? They talk about "experience" quite glibly. Sex is an
experience. LSD, according to all reports, certainly is an

experience. Joining a picket line is an experience. But all of these can be experienced without love, because love brings with it involvement, and involvement means vulnerability.

Tom Bade, a Young Life worker speaking of this fear of personal commitment, said, "If you want experience, go to a prostitute. If you want involvement, get married." He was illustrating in that pungent sentence the truth that love can't be had without involvement, a total commitment of one's whole self. In a sense, to say, "I love you," means, "I take you into my life and I give myself into your life. From now on there will be no unrelated areas, no hidden compartments."

This wholesale commitment of the self is far removed from the glib talk of "love" many moderns use. They have "happenings" — a true description of life in fragments.

We will never put the pieces and fragments together by a process of reasoning through knowledge to love. The path of reason and logic will never lead to love. The New Testament is full of commands that we include knowledge in our love, but there is no hint that love can be discovered by intellect.

The whole tenor of the scriptural message is that commitment comes first and is followed by understanding. "And I pray that you, firmly fixed in love yourselves, may be able to grasp (with all Christians) how wide and deep and long and high is the love of Christ — and to know for yourselves that love so far beyond our comprehension" (Ephesians 3:17-19).

This is affirmed by the witness of Christians in all ages. They tell us, and we may confirm it, that some things can be known, in the sense of experiencing them, without being capable of description. It is this kind of knowledge, rooted in commitment — or worse still, in obedience to God, or to a moral code, or a principle — which is so repugnant to the modern mind. If there were some other way than by going

into it blindly, some kind of chart or blueprint, how easily
we would accept it! The temptation to try and meet this
need by providing a blueprint is very great, but it is at this
point that the Gospel is most unyielding: If anyone will *do*
. . . he will know.

Only the loving will have any understanding of love
— just as only the good will understand goodness. When
one has gotten only a little way into loving, one learns that
what understanding we do attain, poor and partial as it
must be, is not gotten by thinking about it. It comes by
receiving and giving love, as a part of the process of living.

Like any other learning experience in life there is a
starting point to learning about love. We must receive love
before we have any to give; and here is where we en-
counter the first difficulty. Jesus' command to love our
neighbor depends on our love for ourselves. If we have no
love for ourselves, it is not likely we will love anyone else.

"How can I learn to love myself?" was the question
asked by a charming, attractive and outwardly happy career
woman at a discussion group recently. She went on to say
that her problem had always been that she could not feel
she was worth loving, so she could not love herself. This
is not an isolated instance, but a very common problem,
even among Christians.

It is no good telling people they must love themselves
when they can't. One might as well say, "Be strong," to a
sick man, or, "Be beautiful," to a plain girl. The question
here is not, "What is love?" but, "*How* do I love . . . myself
. . . God . . . other people?" The desperation in such a
situation has sent many people to the psychiatrist and the
psychologist, and there is no doubt but that they can help a
great deal. In fact, for some very deep-rooted and complex
problems leading to a lack of self-love, professional help is
imperative.

The Starting Point of Love

The starting point for any valid love of self is *not* what *we* think of ourselves. We are finite creatures prone to error, and we need a more reliable opinion of our worth. We find the estimate of our value stated and restated in the Bible — *God* loves us! That doesn't mean that He approves of us, or admires our characters. It has *nothing* to do with our character or habits. It is concerned with us, with you and me, the real "I" that lies beneath the surface of our personage. That "I" is loved by God.

We can see one evidence of His love for us in the fact that we are all different. God has created an infinite variety of men and women, rather than turning us out like so many cookies from the press. He sees us as persons, as individuals, because He created us that way. It seems reasonable to surmise that if *we* love what we have made — our children, obviously, but also our handiwork — God does too. The artist loves his painting, the gardener dotes on his garden, the writer cherishes his words. In this, we are like God. This kind of love is a faint likeness, and only a likeness, but it helps us to understand how God could love us, His creatures, even in our rebellion.

For God does not love us as mere extensions of His personality. The Bible does not refer merely to creation as evidence that we are loved, but to redemption. "The proof of God's amazing love is this: that it was *while we were sinners* that Christ died for us," said Paul in Romans 5:8 (italics mine). He used the word sinners in the sense of our alienation from God and the whole bent of our nature toward evil, rather than as a description of a kind of behavior. We were God's enemies — but He loved us.

If the statement that God loves us in spite of our indifference and enmity toward Him staggers us, it is usually because we either do not believe we are lovable (I'm so unworthy nobody could love me, least of all God) or that we do not believe we are at odds with God (what have I ever done to Him?). For those in the second category there is plenty of evidence in the Bible regarding human perversity — not to mention our own rare moments of honesty when we look for a horrified second at the meanness, malice, pettiness and spite within us. We know, at such times, that simply to *be* capable of these things is an offense against God.

For the "poor in spirit" who cannot believe anyone would love them, who are only too aware of their sins, there is an equally great weight of evidence regarding God's concern. It is the whole history of God's people, men and women who have given themselves for others for no other reason than God loves — so they love. It reaches from today, from the quiet but tireless missionaries working in unnoticed backwaters, back through the generations to the days of the early church and the apostles' unceasing care for their converts. Back to Jesus, surrounded day after day by needy people, healing them, feeding them, teaching them. Back even farther to the ancient days when the tiny Jewish confederation of tribes, rebellious and stubborn, heard God through the prophets.

The prophet Jeremiah, after describing to the Israelites the anger and judgment of God for their wickedness, and listing their sins from idolatry to immorality, turns and says: "The Lord hath appeared of old unto me, saying, Yea, I have loved thee with an everlasting love: therefore with lovingkindness have I drawn thee" (31:3).

The same emphasis occurs in Moses' reminder to the Israelites that their position as the chosen people of God was not "because ye were more in number than any people; for ye were the fewest of all people: but because the Lord loved you . . ." (Deuteronomy 7:8, 8). Not because we are good or deserving or powerful or gifted but because of His love for us are we His.

There is only one thing we must do and it is the same thing required of those ancient Israelites — we must hear and answer God's call. That is all they did. Some people think that God showed an arbitrary favoritism toward the Jews, making them a sort of teacher's pet among the nations, but the evidence does not bear this out. Abraham heard God's call to come out from the polytheistic culture in which he lived, and his faithfulness to that call made him God's man. It is the same today. God's message to the world is heard by a minority; they are the ones who are willing to become His at the inconvenience of giving up what the rest of the world clings to. Not trivial things, as a superficial view of Christianity suggests, but our right to ourselves; that is, our right to put ourselves in the center of our world, ignoring God and others except as they are useful to us. *That* attitude leads to some very scandalous sins, but in itself it is worse than any of them.

Learning to Be Loved

Since God loves us because He is love and not because we are especially deserving, it follows that we are then free to love ourselves. *Who are we to despise what God loves?*

For some of us the fact that God loves us, knowing what we are, is difficult to accept because all the love we have ever known has been conditioned on our good behavior. I have known parents whose idea of discipline was to punish their children by cold disapproval: "You naughty child, Mother doesn't love you when you behave like that!" When one has learned very early in life that to displease Mother can turn her face into a mask of dislike — even of rejection — it is very hard to believe that God, so much more distant and fearful in His heaven, loves unconditionally.

All our lives we are being taught, not deliberately and calculatingly, but by example, by observation of the way people treat each other, that we must *earn* love. I can't remember when it was that I began to be hurt at indifference, but it was very early. I knew, as I think all children "just know," that when my parents or friends were angry it was because I'd done something they didn't like. Anyone can understand that. But indifference, simply being ignored — that was far worse, that really cut deeply, because it meant that I was not even worthy of irritation, unimportant, too worthless to be cross with. Now I suspect that that undefined, but very real, appreciation of both anger and indifference (which is rejection) is universal. We know that anger doesn't negate love, but we know that to be ignored is to be unloved.

We learn as children that other children "like" us when we give them their way, when we let them choose the game, when we share our toys. We see that our elders are pleased with us when we do what we're told and don't make a mess or noise or bother them. We see that the whole adult world, from teachers and parents to aunts and uncles, can be friendly toward us when we do things their way, and we get the message: I must please others if I want to be loved. We learn to behave the way the adults want us to because we need to be loved, and we learn that certain kinds of naughtiness bring wrath and punishment upon us — but other misdeeds bring total rejection. Anger directed at *what we've done* we can understand — it will pass; but indifference means that *what we are* is unacceptable.

That is why the Old Testament often portrays God as angry, fearfully and thunderingly angry with His children, but *never* disinterested. He may punish them, He would never ignore them. *Anger is not the thing that betrays our lack of love, but indifference.*

For those unfortunates who have grown up under the

shadow of a warped and muddied version of love it is almost inconceivable to believe God loves us when we are perverse, or cold toward Him, or deliberately disobedient. We may read the words in the Bible, but the long-established climate of our lives makes its truth foreign to us. Our emotions fail to digest what the intellect accepts. What is the cure for this?

Certainly there is no magic formula that will do the trick. Once the truth of the Gospel has been accepted, all our thinking has to be brought into conformity with it. The old, habitual set of mind, which we have been all our lives acquiring, does not fall away overnight. It must be *pushed out* by something new. So we find Paul advising the Christians in Rome (and certainly their pagan frame of mind must have needed revamping) to "let God remold your minds from within . . ." (12:2). That is exactly the procedure for learning to accept God's love. We read the Bible, and, as we read, the unfamiliar concepts begin to find a place in our thinking. We pray, telling Him of our sins — and our feelings of unworthiness, and even (for He knows it already) of our secret fears that He could not possibly love us after *this* particular failure. We learn slowly, day by day, to grow up into Christian maturity which means first of all being loved by God. We will never have enough love, except our poor version, to give to others unless we accept God's love for us.

And that, too, must be learned. No doubt it would be wonderful if, right from the beginning of our Christian lives, we were filled with a glorious certainty of His love and could float along on a wave of emotional euphoria. But for most of us this is not the way it will be.

On the days when we are doing well — in fact, feeling quite "spiritual" — it will be easy to think God loves us. But when we have been caught in some instinctive reaction and committed a mean, petty little sin which embarrasses us every time it comes to mind — then it will be hard. Like disobedient children expecting the stern, unloving gaze of Faher's displeasure, we will feel unloved, because we are undeserving. At such times our only safety lies in turning instantly to God for forgiveness — forgiveness offered in love, and offered freely. We may not feel forgiven, or loved, but we accept it. Slowly, and with many setbacks and misgivings, we learn to be loved. The climate of our lives is changing.

But there are pitfalls we must avoid.

There are those — and most of us are prone to do it — who, unlike the "poor in spirit," are always bemoaning the fact that *we too* need His forgiveness. What seems to be self-condemnation, a deep sense of sin, is really the most obsessive kind of pride. We cannot bear to accept God's forgiveness and go on from there because we cannot bear to accept our own sinfulness. You know the sort of self-castigation this attitude produces: "I'll *never* forgive myself for such a thing! Why, I've never even thought of such things before. To think that *I* should sink so low!" The only real emotion here is a humiliation born out of pride. The secret thought behind it is: "How could I, of all people, do such a thing! I am really above such miserable sins, and I cannot face knowing that I am really no better than those other wretches."

The saddest part of this particular attitude is that it shuts out the love of God like an iron door. The poor in spirit, who have a hard time understanding God's love because no one has ever really loved them, may eventually accept it as little children accept an unexpected gift, but the secretly proud and arrogant cannot accept it because it is offered only to the unworthy — and they are unwilling to take it on those terms.

The whole history of God's chosen people is the story of their reluctance, which is also our reluctance, simply to

receive God's love. He gave them the Law to live by, a
guidepost which surely ought to have constantly reminded
them of their inability and failure to keep it. They began
to imagine that they not only kept the Law, but they in-
vented refinements on it to add to their attainments. He
gave them the land they lived in and they soon felt they
had gotten it for themselves — and no more than they deserved, either!

But before we begin to congratulate ourselves that *we*
see *their* mistakes all too plainly, let us be reminded that
we do the same thing. God has given us His Spirit to
guide, comfort, and correct us, and we begin to congratulate ourselves on our spiritual sensitivity. He gave us the
Church because we need each other, and we have walled it
off and divided it into hundreds of tiny compounds, deciding who is and is not "really" Christian. He gave us the
Bible to teach us, and we use it like a bludgeon to beat each
other over the head with; and we quote Scripture verses to
wound instead of to heal.

Worst of all, we have become "respectable." We talk,
in our Christian groups, about being sinners, but with the
mental reservation that there are, thank goodness, some sins
which we certainly would not be guilty of. No doubt God
forgives those who do sin, we mentally add, but though we
may meet them in heaven (suitably cleaned up, we trust)
we need not mingle with them here.

This very point was discussed once in a Bible study
group of young married women. One of them remarked
that, to God, sin is sin and He makes no difference between
gossip and backbiting and adultery. The subject of social
sins was thoroughly analyzed and everyone concluded
that God certainly did forgive those sins just as He forgave
"our" little everyday meannesses. And then one young wife
said, "Of course, *we* wouldn't do anything like that."

Wouldn't we? As long as we cherish the illusion that

we have any virtue in ourselves, we are no candidates for God's love. That is for those who need Him, who cannot do without Him and who know it.

But for those who need Him and *don't know it* — the respectable, moral, righteous people — the shock of finding themselves fallen into some common flagrant sin is too much. That is why some Christians end up in despair over their failures, unable to accept God's forgiveness because they are enraged at really needing it. All that parrot talk about sin really didn't mean a thing. John the Baptist came preaching repentance and the religious leaders called him a fanatic. But Jesus turned on them and said, "Yes, and I tell you that tax collectors and prostitutes are going into the kingdom of God in front of you. For John came to you as a saint, and you did not believe him — yet the tax collectors and the prostitutes did! And, even after seeing that, you would not change your minds and believe him" (Matthew 21:32).

In the same vein He told Simon, a *very* respectable and religious man, that the woman of the streets, prostrated in her repentance, was forgiven. "For she has shown me so much love. But the man who has little to be forgiven has only a little love to give" (Luke 7:47). This was a subtle way of telling Simon — and all of us like him — that anyone who imagines that he has few sins to be forgiven is blind to his own sinfulness, and therefore blind to the love of God which is offered to everyone.

Do we want love in our lives? God offers it to us, a measureless ocean of love. Even if no one has ever loved us, He does. There is nothing we can do that will put us beyond it. The only thing that can keep us from it is any illusion that we deserve it. His love is limitless — it is free — and it is unearned.

2. LOVE
IN
ACTION

This love of which I speak is slow to lose patience — it looks for a way of being constructive.   — I Corinthians 13:4

When I was first a Christian and had accepted God's love for me, I expected to be able immediately to love everyone around me. It was a crushing blow to discover that I couldn't. The same people irritated me who had irritated me before. I prayed about my lack of love — and nothing happened. To those who loved me, I responded with love, but I found the same difficulty loving the unloving I had known before. What was wrong? Where were the feelings of benevolence toward everyone that a Christian was supposed to have?

Ah, there was the trouble. I expected to have my *feelings* changed, and that is not how God works. I supposed He would change my feelings, because I thought of myself as being whatever my feelings were at any moment. That is just not true. I am not my feelings any more than I am what I ate for dinner last night. Our feelings may be very much the result of what we ate for dinner, but neither feelings nor food determine what we are. A temporary mood *is* determined by feeling when we act on no other basis than feeling — but usually we do not, fortunately. In our daily lives we get up and go through the day for other reasons than feelings, although our attitude may be modified by feeling. Why, since nothing else we do is determined by our feelings, should we expect our Christian lives to be based on that?

"But Christianity is founded on love," the new convert might protest, "and love is — well, love is a feeling." No, indeed, that is just what love is not. Love may result in a feeling, but it is not that alone, just as you and I are more than the sum total of our feelings. When we mistake our "loving feelings" for love, we are mistaking the effect for the cause.

Love is passionate concern for someone; it is delight in that person — a desire to please, often a longing to possess, a need to know and be known. It is a need for, and a wish to be needed. But love is more than all these things, and all these things may not be good. The passionate concern may be jealous and exclusive. The longing to possess may be selfish, the need for the loved one may be warped. Are these the things the Bible is talking about? Surely not. Then what *is* the love it is so full of — a love we find so elusive?

Love Is Not Feeling

It is possible that for all our contemporary chatter about love, we know very little about it. Believing it to be a feeling, we pursue it fruitlessly, since feelings are always fading. The truth is that we tend to describe everything in terms of the shallowest part of our experience — our emotions

— so we are always making the same mistake. We *think* our feelings are love, or peace, or good will, when actually they are only by-products of those qualities. Besides being the "nerve-response" to far deeper attitudes of will and heart, our feelings are conditioned by our health, our digestion, and the state of the weather, among other things.

The Bible never speaks of love in such terms. *Love is always described in action* in the Bible. Reluctant as we may be to accept it, the truth is that a great many of the most important experiences we have simply cannot be classified or defined the way we describe an object — by merely appending a list of adjectives. Therefore the Bible pictures love for us, not in terms of adjectives but of action — what love does how it behaves. Jesus told His disciples that their love for Him would be demonstrated when they kept His commandments; when they did good not evil to their enemies. He told them that His love for them would be supremely validated as He laid down His life for them.

It seems then that the Biblical concept of love is different from our idea of it as an emotion. We might say it is *more than* an emotion. How do we find out what love is for ourselves?

A mother awakened at night by her child's cry, getting up in the chill of early morning to hold and comfort him, is too tired for emotion. But the love is there. Every tired father, coming home from work, longing for the evening paper and his easy chair but instead whipping up enthusiasm for a tussle with his son, knows the difference between the emotion and the reality of love. The reality spurs one on when the emotion is buried under fatigue.

The reality underlying both emotion and action, the inner set of mind and attitude is what Jesus is referring to when He says, "If any one wants to *do* God's will, he will *know* whether my teaching is from God or whether I merely speak on my own authority."

When the Bible speaks of love behaving a certain way, doing this and not that, having this attitude, not that, it is really showing us how to obey the command to love. First we obey, perhaps feeling nothing of the warmth we had hoped would be ours — no overflowing zeal for God, no concern for man. We simply do what we are told with nothing more to go on than the words of the Bible and our will to be faithful to what God has commanded. Only afterwards do we begin to experience something of the warm tide of feeling and emotion flowing through us.

This is as it should be. The only love we have to give others is what God gives us, and it appears very much as though His giving is based on our obedience to His commands. "Do, and you will know."

As we look for direction from the Bible, we find that all the passages speaking of love weave themselves together in a most remarkable way. (See the Glossary of Love on pp. 187ff.) For the purposes of our discussion we are using the 13th chapter of I Corinthians. These words which have become a classic piece of literature on love occur in the middle of a letter written to the Christians at Corinth primarily to chastise them for their scandalous behavior and to instruct them in the kind of life God expected of them.

After reprimanding them severely for their quarrels and cliques and foolish pride over whatever spiritual "gifts" they enjoyed, Paul told them that love surpasses all these gifts and launched into a magnificent and poetic passage in praise of love. The poetry is immediately followed, however, by a lengthy list of the acts and attitudes of love. As we read them, the little word "love" begins to acquire flesh and blood and spirit.

Love Cannot Be Cut Off

This love of which I speak is slow to lose patience — it looks for a way of being constructive.

What an odd way to begin defining love! Patience is not an attribute that is especially admired or desired today. We think of it in terms of the old, who are patient because everything worth being impatient for is behind them; or the dull, who are too thick-witted to realize the necessity of action. To a culture that is speeded up and rushing forward (though to what end we may not know) the concept of patience seems as mid-Victorian as antimacassars. But is it?

One of the friends my husband and I have had for a long time is a person of extremely high and rigid moral standards; not that our other friends don't have high principles, but this woman's standards keep her at a tension all the time. I suspect she may be secretly nervous about failing to meet those standards. She holds them up, not only for herself, but for all her friends. Several times in the years we have known her she has abruptly cut a friendship off because someone has come a cropper — failed to meet the demands of the standard.

"She knew what she was doing was wrong," my friend said once in discussing another woman. "I have no patience with people like that. I always say, if you can't be helpful to a person, then why bother with them, and I certainly tried to be helpful to her."

My own attitude toward this friend is very wary; I feel our relationship rests on extremely shaky ground. I don't anticipate going out and committing any grave sins, but her idea of acceptable behavior differs from mine. Since she is so critical and impatient with everyone, what will happen if I fail to behave exactly as she thinks I should? There is no durability to her affection for anyone. Her impatience with people cuts off affection for them if they ever disappoint her. Love — and certainly friendship is a kind of love — to be worth anything at all must have durability to it or it is nothing.

The patience Paul is talking about isn't the kind which

means we must never, however tired we are, utter a cross word (though it is highly desirable not to, since any situation deteriorates when tempers are short). It is the kind of patience which never gives up. People who are so lacking in patience that they are always breaking relationships are the most unrealistic souls on earth. Who of us is beyond sin? Who is there who doesn't at one time or another fall short as a Christian and as a friend? Only that person who never fails has the right to be impatient with others — but I don't know anyone like that, and neither do you.

No, a person who lacks patience with others — and often with himself, as well — can never sustain a lasting relationship with anyone because no one will ever be able to meet his demand for perfection. Such a person has always to convince himself that he *is* living up to his standards, which means he is constantly pretending to himself, excusing and rationalizing his own lapses from perfection; or else he must be always sunk in self-condemnation. There are people like that. They don't like anyone, but they don't like themselves either.

Without patience *no* virtue at all is real. If whatever virtues we possess melt away at the least frustration or disappointment — if we haven't the patience to keep on — then they are no more substantial than ice in the sun. While there are other words for the kind of patience we are describing: endurance, forbearance, longsuffering, none of them says quite the same thing, but there are elements of all of them in patience, and more. The patience we need to maintain any relationship is one which looks expectantly for the good in people. Without that kind of optimism, if you want to call it that, forbearance can be a bit grim — a dull, resigned kind of tolerance that has a very bad effect on the one who practices it. Endurance without optimism causes us, if we allow it to make its home in our lives, to be spurious heroes and heroines.

I once knew a woman who was constantly doing good to people. She found no task too much, if someone needed help. Yet somehow or other it seemed that the recipients of her kindness always turned out to be unworthy of it. She would relate to her friends some tale of ingratitude on the part of the person she was trying to help, then sigh and say, "We must just pray for her. The Lord knows, I've talked and talked, showed her what the Scripture says, and I've tried to help her see what's right. I've certainly gone the second mile, and I'm willing to go on indefinitely if the Lord wants it, but. . . ." Her friends were supposed to say, "Oh, Helen, you're so wonderful, I just don't see how you can put up with someone like that." The truth of the matter was that Helen lost patience the moment her "projects" showed the least sign of behaving like real people instead of cardboard dolls. Her attitude of longsuffering patience was really a mask for a deadly kind of impatience. Real patience would have been able to go on being helpful in spite of set-backs.

Patience, like all other virtues, is never called upon until the situation provokes its opposite. The very word calls up pictures of events which make us impatient. Who needs patience when everything is going our way, when all the people and events in our lives unroll as smoothly as a red carpet before us? We only need it when something happens that normally makes for impatience. The whole list of Christian virtues is predicated upon a world which usually makes these virtues difficult.

We have only to give the most cursory glance at history to realize that mankind is self-seeking, perverse, of uncertain virtue, and often stupid. It is these tendencies in us that call forth patience in all our relationships. Impatience has provoked lovers' quarrels, estrangement between parents and children, political upheaval, and, of course, war between nations. No relationship can thrive without a liberal quantity of patience from at least one of those involved, and hopefully from more than one.

A friend of mine, a teacher, said once that the secret of success in her field lay in being able to tell the student the same thing time after time without ever becoming impatient. All of us are indebted, in some way, to this kind of patience for all we have learned.

I remember once, some years ago, coming back from a conference in the mountains full of enthusiasm over a new concept of Christian living I'd heard from one of the speakers. As I related this wonderful new discovery to my friend and pastor, Dr. Richard C. Halverson, I became aware of an odd expression on his face. Finally he said sadly, "I've been telling you that very same thing for years."

A moment's silence fell, while I thought back on some of the truths he'd been talking about in Bible study groups, and I knew what had happened. He had taught me, patiently and without reproach for my density, telling me the thing I needed to know over and over again, sometimes by stories, approaching it from every angle. And then a dramatic message by another man brought it all into focus for me for the first time. That flash of insight would never have occurred if Dick hadn't persisted, with the utmost patience, in telling me the same thing again and again. Like Paul, he planted — someone else watered — but God gave the increase. The insight was born out of patience.

Love Makes Allowances

When a lover says to his beloved, "I'll love you forever," he'd better mean, "I'll be patient forever," because without a large measure of patience the love won't last long. Do you see how very necessary are all these qualifications and descriptions of how love acts? And patience is only the first in quite a long list! Paul advised the Christians at Ephesus to, "accept life with humility and patience, making allowance for each other because you love each other." The woman I mentioned earlier, who certainly made no allowances for anyone, who cut off her friends without compunction if they failed to meet her standards, that woman never loved. Love can hardly exist for one day without patience, not to mention surviving the ups and downs of a sustained relationship. The phrase, "making allowance," is a nice brief way of saying, "taking into consideration all of original sin, inherited weakness and acquired evil that goes into each one of us." That kind of compassionate forbearance is required of us if love is to be part of our lives.

I haven't mentioned yet the obvious example of parent-hood as a demand for patience. Every one of us must sadly admit that we have often been impatient and have been sorry about it afterwards. Now that my children are grown, the thing I regret most about the years they were growing up is that I wasn't more patient. Like many of you I was often tired, and fatigue breeds impatience; I was anxious for my children to behave well; and, reluctantly, I must admit that I didn't want them to cause me any extra trouble. You know the sort of thing — "Donna, not *again*. That's the second shoe you've lost outside. You just go right out and find it!"

A certain amount of impatience in such situations is inevitable. No doubt there would be something highly un-natural about a mother who never raised her voice or took the smile off her face. And yet we all know that we are often cross when we shouldn't be. We are impatient because our children are behaving like children and not like adults.

It is just here where the habit of making allowances helps us most. We remind ourselves that, after all, they *are* children; and from a child's point of view a lot of the things that irritate parents seem perfectly right and logical. Like Donna's habit of losing her shoes outside. On warm days her little feet got hot and cramped, and the shoes were obviously contributing to that discomfort. So why not take them off? Toes are for wiggling in the dust, and one can't do that with shoes on.

Love Is For Real — People That Is

If we were really honest with ourselves, we would have to admit that a great deal of our impatience with people stems from a wholly illogical conviction that they must see the situation from our viewpoint and are deliberately being obstructive or annoying. We do it all the time with our children; we assume that they, with their childish minds, understand what they are doing as we understand it. We do it with other people, imposing our particular view of life upon them in our thinking with no regard for them as real people at all. Genuine, unadulterated *impatience* flourishes only in the sour soil of egotism. The merest breath of honesty shows its sour character at once.

The egotist sees himself as the center of the world — and, of course, in the center of God's truth. Other people are seen as more or less dim figures, depending upon their conformity to the egotist's own arbitrary standards, which he assumes must also be God's standards. That is why he is so impatient with people: can't they *see* how wrong they are in failing to live up to the divinely given truth, as exemplified in himself?

Do you begin to see why Paul, in describing love, starts with patience? Patience as a virtue becomes real to us when we see that we are what we are because God Himself has expended an inexhaustible amount of patience on us. We are where we are, within the circle of His love, because of His bearing with us, a patience which is part of His love. How can we be impatient with others for failing to meet our requirements, when (painful though it is to admit it) we are not able to meet them ourselves, much less meet the perfection which God demands? When we are able honestly to face our own failure to satisfy the smallest command of God's law, and to see ourselves *as we are* — poor, imperfect creatures drawing every breath by the love and forbearance of God — then we can begin to be patient with others.

Matthew, reliving the days when he watched Jesus teach and heal, and writing his careful record for the struggling church, remembered Isaiah's words about the Messiah who was to come: "A bruised reed shall he not break, and smoking flax shall he not quench" (12:20). The picture these words call up is of a Man who carefully nurtures the wounded, who encourages the least sign of life in the almost-dead fire. We get a different picture, but the same meaning in the words of Jesus Himself: "In any case I did not come to invite the 'righteous' but the 'sinners' " (Matthew 9:13).

As long as we imagine ourselves to be "the righteous," those whom God is quite fortunate to have among His followers, we can indulge in all kinds of impatience with "those others," who can't seem to manage life as well as we do. The image is as insubstantial as our reflection in a pool of water, however; the moment a rock is tossed into the pool the image shatters (and life is full of rocks). We must face the truth: *we* are the bruised reeds, and the smoking flax. Our little lives depend for their every minute upon the patience of God. Who are we to be impatient with others?

Now we see why patience is a necessary part of love. We can only love real people — not projected images of ourselves in other people; *real people do not think, act, talk, exactly like we do.* Patience is the quality which closes the gap between ourselves and others. It is a kind of heavenly courtesy which says, "I do not quite understand why you are as you are, but then I cannot understand myself; and since there is One who understands us both, let us extend to each other the patience He has had for each of us." Love without patience is not really love at all, but a shadowy vapor which will vanish at the first hot wind of reality, as the mists of night vanish when morning comes.

Love Is Constructive

Paul qualifies his mention of patience with these words: "It looks for a way of being constructive." The phrase adds color and depth and lightness to the picture of patience. One might, in thinking of a patient person, imagine a woman never flurried, always serene; someone gently smiling, unshaken by irritation or impetuousness. Possibly the picture, though sweet, is a little flat. We sense a kind of passivity in it.

That is not the image Paul is bringing to life at all. He pictures patience at work with the sparkle and excitement of action — it looks for a way of being constructive. There is none of the gentle half-smile of resignation or passive acceptance here. The words convey a sense of vigor, of briskness, of movement.

We see this illustrated most perfectly in the mother with her child just learning to walk. He staggers wildly from table to chair, often losing his balance and sitting down abruptly, but his mother picks him up and starts him off again. She doesn't expect perfection at once, but she keeps him headed in that direction — as far as walking is concerned. That is, in brief, the whole story of his life — trying something new, falling, trying again, finally achieving. Mother is always there to pick him up when he falls, to encourage him, to keep him facing the direction he ought to go. That is the kind of patience and constructive help the word "Mother" means to us — or ought to.

Unfortunately, not all mothers are like that with their children. One woman I know always has seemed to assume that the way to make her children do their best is to accuse them, in highly unrealistic and passionate terms, of the most extreme kind of determined wickedness. Her opening gambit usually goes something like this:

"Mike! *Mike!* Come in here this instant! Look at this room — just look at it! No wonder I'm so tired I'm half sick, when I work so hard to keep this place decent and you deliberately mess it up as fast as I can clean it. You like to see me worn to a frazzle, don't you? You can run off and play while I'm trying to do the work of ten women. You can remember to go off with your friends but you can *never* remember to pick up your clothes. Did you carry out the trash this morning like your Dad told you? No, you never think of things like that, do you?" And on and on and on.

The children are not the only ones on the receiving end of this tactic. There are women whose attitude toward their husbands is always, "You never take me anywhere nice," or, "Joan's husband bought her a fur cape for her birthday. Why don't you ever think of something nice for me? You never even remember my birthday."

If we are completely, painfully honest with ourselves we will admit that we all have a little bit of the whiner in us. I think the people who are constantly accusing others of terrible, deliberate and magnified failures must think that by so exaggerating their complaint the recipient will be stung into proving them wrong by doing the opposite. Of course that never happens.

What does happen is that the ones accused grow so accustomed to the barrage of propaganda that they never hear it at all, or else they begin to be what they are accused of being. All of us respond in some way to what others think of us and expect of us. Encouragement and trust inspires us to become what others expect of us. When we are told, day after day after day, that we are lazy or stupid or ugly, we become that.

We are all, far more than we realize, putting something

of ourselves into other people and being similarly altered by them. No doubt that is why the New Testament so frequently portrays the Church as a body, organically tied together as a physical body is. When John Donne said, "No man is an island, entire of itself," that's what he meant. We all know that is true, but I think some of us regard it as a mystical truth, or possibly a theological truth, by which we mean it isn't really so at all but is just a nice way of saying we ought to be good to each other.

In fact, both the Bible and John Donne are describing a validity: we are *really*, not figuratively, giving something of ourselves and receiving from others, both altering and being altered. I am not speaking of some kind of merging of selves, or blurring of identity, but of the inescapable truth that we, by our attitudes and words and actions, are constantly "making" each other better or worse. There is the awkward, clumsy girl whose parents have always scolded her for her clumsiness. She is constantly hearing, "Pick *up* your feet, Judy. I've never seen anyone as bumbling as you are. Hold your head up, don't slouch so. For heaven's sake, don't *fidget*, learn to keep your hands still." Poor child, how could she think of herself as anything but awkward? It's been dinned into her for so long that it has become a part of her.

Children are the most vulnerable to the judgments of their elders, for they have no experience to go on yet that would balance what they are told. How many are all their lives children inwardly, believing they are stupid, or lazy, or homely, because they've been told it so many times?

On the other hand, many of us can look back with thankfulness to the people who encouraged us to become better than we were. They were, whether they knew it or not, fulfilling this Biblical command to look for a way of being constructive. As I look back upon twenty-seven years of marriage I can see that I am the person I am today because of a great many people, but chiefly because of my husband. The timidity and fear of new situations which had always been part of me began to melt away (though it took years) because he always told me, "Go ahead — you can do it." He thought I was a good cook and a good housekeeper and a good seamstress, and under his approval I began to be. He told me I could write. For years I chuckled at that, knowing within myself that I "really couldn't." But he told me and told me, and badgered me, and finally I began to do a little writing. Then others came along who encouraged me. But without the constant assurance of my husband, no amount of encouragement from others would have done it.

Of course, this way of being constructive cannot be based on a mere flight of fancy. Russ *never* encouraged me to be a singer — he knew very well I couldn't carry a tune. The important thing to remember is that every one of us has certain qualities of character and personality, certain abilities and tastes, which will blossom with encouragement and may wither under disparagement.

Let us be very careful that the mark we are making on other people is good and helpful and constructive. If it is, it will be permanent, because it goes on into eternity.

It is becoming quite apparent why the word "love" alone is not enough. We must know that it is patient, and not quick to discard; that it is constructive, building good things into those it touches rather than magnifying weakness. Like everything that is real and true, this love has its imitations: pale, warped, and insubstantial as smoke, these poor travesties of love may delude us into thinking they are real by the emotion with which they flare up. Emotions come and go. Love, the love the Bible describes, remains when emotions are gone.

Love is the fuel that gets us out of bed to fix breakfast when we would rather turn over and go to sleep. It sends many a man off to work when his mood tells him to chuck it. Nothing but love keeps parents serene when their almost-grown children are brash and contemptuous of their standards. And if you feel your patience has been tried beyond all reason — remember, *the cross marks the limit of God's patience toward us.* It is a limit too high for us to pass, and so vast it puts our own strained patience back into perspective.

3. LOVE
WITHOUT
GREED

Love . . . is not possessive.   — I Corinthians 13:4

Love is not possessive! What a contradiction in terms this seems to be! To love is to want to possess, at least in this world. We are even repelled by the idea of a love which wants nothing for itself — it smacks of milk-and-water, impossibly goody-goody attitudes.

For a generation raised on the idea of the virtue of aggressiveness and brought up to admire strength and the sheer thrust of force strong enough to overcome all obstacles, this definition of love offers nothing we want. A love that seeks nothing for itself seems to be purely negative, and we long for our lives to be filled with positive good.

Paul's phrase, "It is not possessive," does not, I think, denote the wan, colorless kind of renunciation we usually associate with bad Victorian novels. There is a proper response to love, but possessiveness implies more than seeking that response. To possess is to own. Ownership means that *this* is mine; I can do with it what I will, I need not share it with anyone, nor consider its desires, for it is mine. Possession is used of things, not people. It turns the object of love into just that — an object, to be handled or put away, enjoyed or rejected, at the whim of the owner.

Two things must be said about a love that is not possessive before we can go further. The first is that natural, instinctive love is of itself possessive. When Paul speaks of a love that is not possessive he is talking about a love that is *not* natural, or instinctive, but supernatural in its being because we do not have it in ourselves. This comes from God. The second is that all natural loves tend to die, or to destroy the very thing they are fastened on, if they are not in some sense redeemed and lifted by this supernatural love which God gives. It is an instance of "common grace" that so many natural loves, outside the Christian faith, are influenced by a higher love.

Love Does Not Dictate

Some time ago I knew a woman who was the victim of a mother's love so possessive that it was destroying the daughter as a person. In her thirties and unmarried, she had never been able to develop any kind of relationship with a man which might have led to marriage because her mother would not allow it. Oh, the mother "loved" her daughter too much to see her continue any further with this or that young man who was too unspiritual — or too crude — or came from a *most* unsuitable background. Her subtle criticisms of all her daughter's friends conveyed disapproval in the most delicate possible chilliness. She advised her daughter kindly about her choice of clothes, hair styles, places to go, subjects to study in school, and insisted that she not wear make-up of any kind. The result was that the poor girl finally had no friends, was afraid to choose her clothes, and lived in terror of her mother's frown.

Of course she was spineless — some women would have revolted, long ago. But think of this treatment begun when she was a tiny child, and continued with no let-up year after year after year. It is quite likely that if she had had the temperament to rebel against such domination, her rebellion would have been as extreme and destructive as her compliance. But her mother did it all out of love — Christian love, she said quite often. At the time I knew the daughter she was pathetically neurotic, and one could see the inevitable breakdown coming. No doubt it was a horrible shock to her mother that one so carefully nurtured, so guided and so restrained from any possible contaminating influence, should be so ungrateful as to have a nervous breakdown.

It is fairly obvious to most of us that we ought not, however much we are inclined, to keep our children bound to us forever. Yet without admitting what we are doing, though we do not carry it so far as the mother I've just mentioned, we often try to possess them in ways that no human can ever possess another. When they are little we tell them what is right and wrong. They start by having the opinions we taught them to have and much of the process of education consists in their learning to think for themselves. When they do think and arrive at conclusions different from the things we have taught them, our reactions go all the way from mild astonishment to furious indignation.

The plain truth is, we *cannot* possess their minds. And if we do succeed in keeping them bound to our thinking, we have only done what tyrants do with drugs — we have brainwashed them. The mind which only thinks what it is told to is less than it was meant to be; the end result of such control — however virtuous the thoughts it is "given" to think — is always destructive. In order for a child to grow up into a whole person, he must think for himself. That process involves making decisions, choices, value judgments and commitments.

While we ought to do all we can to help our children love the truth, to think logically and to commit themselves to God for His purposes, we must also do them the honor of allowing them to be whole persons. And that means that, however earnestly we guide them, in the end they *do it themselves*. Besides, none of us has a corner on all the truth there is. We tend to think we have — that our grasp of things is absolute, which is ridiculous. I may know the truth about many things, but I do not know all of it; and especially I do not know all of God's truth. It is a human tendency, though not a good one, to endeavor to make absolutes out of relative truths and insist that others accept our thinking as divinely inspired. For that reason, it may be a very good thing that our children do not always accept our teaching blindly.

The mother who tearfully says, "But it's because I love you so much, that I want you to believe this . . . accept that . . . behave this way," is speaking out of her purely natural and instinctive love, a love which says, "This is mine and it will be what I want it to be, where I want it to be." If she should succeed in keeping her child completely tied to her, she will destroy the whole person and end up with a robot. No, there is *no way* we can insure our children's obedience to our teaching. That little baby will grow up to be a man or woman who must make his own choices before God, and we cannot do it for him.

This fact makes us very fearful. How are we going to be sure that our children grow up to believe in what is right, and make the choices that lead to life and not death? The love that the Bible commands us to have cannot be superimposed on someone like one of those glass covers the Victorians put over their flower arrangements to maintain them in a state of constant perfection. It can only be shown,

the way we offer a gift on our open hand, a gift which may
be accepted or rejected. Or, to put it another way, *love can
be lived.* This is really what Jesus meant when He said,
"You will be witnesses to me." What we teach our children
is constantly being either confirmed or invalidated by the
way we live. Love which is implicit in us — part of our
being so that it "just comes out" in our lives — is the guaran-
tee that what we teach our children is true. Of course we
pray for them. God does not operate in a void, however,
and we are part of the material He works with; our lives,
our attitudes, are offered up with our prayers whether we
know it or not.

Love Is Constant

The love given to us by God and which transforms
and translates our purely earthly love is a constant factor in a shifting world. Everything changes — people alter, situations evolve into new combinations, nothing stays
the same. A love which is based on nothing more than the
instinctive desire to possess will change and diminish with
the flux of circumstance. It was fixed on the appearance
and not the substance of the person, impaled on a moment
of time and when that moment dissolved and the object of
love changed, as we all do, the love vanished. Shakespeare
knew this; one of his sonnets, although it is addressed to
love between man and woman, is a true description of love
transformed by the grace of God.

> Let me not to the marriage of true minds
> Admit impediments. Love is not love
> Which alters when it alterations finds,
> Or bends with the remover to remove.
> O, no! it is an ever-fixèd mark
> That looks on tempests, and is never shaken;
> It is the star to every wandering bark,

Whose worth's unknown, although his height be taken.
Love's not Time's fool, though rosy lips and cheeks
Within his bending sickle's compass come;
Love alters not with his brief hours and weeks,
But bears it out even to the edge of doom.
    If this be error, and upon me proved,
    I never writ, nor no man ever loved.

Love does not change with the alteration of our lives only when we do not possess the people we love. When we possess a thing, when we've gotten it to the place we think it's perfect, we want it to stay that way. But no human relationship "stays that way," because the people in it are always changing — especially children.

Haven't you heard mothers who said with a sigh, "Now that David's started dating he just doesn't have time for his Mother any more"? Of course not. Why should he? One doesn't have dates with one's mother, and for a woman to expect to occupy the bulk of her son's time and thought is positively unwholesome. The proper function of a parent is to prepare children for life in their own sphere. As they grow to maturity and need us less, we begin to withdraw — not from their love, not from their lives, but certainly from the forefront. The love between parents and children remains, but it adapts itself to new functions, required by the alterations of time. When love cannot do this, it reveals itself as unredeemed by Christ, and becomes ruinous. "Mother" is not the same as "Wife," and the love expressed and received by women in *either* role is never competitive.

Now that my son and daughter are both married, they still love me as their mother — marriage doesn't change that. Nor has it diminished my love for them. What *has* been changed is the context in which our mutual love is expressed. They no longer need me to care for their physical needs, to supervise their lives and to discipline them. That element is gone from our relationship, but something much richer has come in its place — friendship. We find new delights in each other as we meet each other with mutual respect as adults. The old parental relationship has not gone, but it has been changed, and for the better. No longer a matter of their need and my responsibility, our love for each other is invested with a new spiritual awareness of one another as human beings.

Furthermore, and best of all, my daughter-in-law and my son-in-law have added to and enriched the whole relationship. As Linda and Darrell and Donna and Mike grow in their love for each other, they help each other to become more mature persons — and that helps me. The old cliché, "You haven't lost a daughter, but gained a son," is *really* true. We have all been added to, and all of us find that the new "in-law" relationship has enriched our old mother-son, mother-daughter relationships. If this sounds fanciful — if you find yourself skeptical of such delight in the marriage of a son or daughter — ask yourself whether it is because your love for your children is so possessive you are unwilling to share them.

Married Love Is Limited

Since God has enough love to go around (speaking in human terms) and we are able to love because He has given us the capacity to love, our love, too, is not a quantitative thing. "But," someone may say at this point, "you are forgetting love between a man and a woman. Now *that* is certainly limited and possessive, and furthermore God intended it that way. One man to one woman was His plan. The Bible plainly says so."

This is a valid point. But here it might be well to look for a moment at the Biblical view of marriage and love. Marriage, in the Biblical sense, is a qualified kind of love, which means that the relationship, as God meant it to be, is the structure within which sexual love between a man and a woman is expressed.

The Biblical view of sexual love is that it is the way love between the sexes is expressed most fully. It is a whole-hearted giving of oneself to another person, a surrender so complete that it can be realized most perfectly only in the context of a permanent relationship. This total giving of oneself to another is not an isolated act, but a continuous offering. It *belongs* to the relationship of love in which two people are one marriage; living together and growing together in the dailiness of life. After the act of love comes sleep, then getting up and going to work, planning together, building together, sometimes suffering together — all the intertwining of the marriage relationship. Sexual love without the total commitment of marriage is common, of course; it always has been. But it is an aberration of the pattern, not the pattern itself — and it is fraught with trouble for those who try its thorny road.

We see this clearly in Jesus' answer to the test question posed to Him by the Pharisees, who wanted to know about the legality of divorce (Matthew 19:1-12). Jesus referred them to the Old Testament: God created humans male and female. "For this cause shall a man leave his father and mother, and shall cleave to his wife; and the twain shall become one flesh." Jesus' commentary was, "So they are no longer two separate people but one. No man therefore must separate what God has joined together."

It is rather thought-provoking to realize that nothing has been said yet about love. Love may be implied, but what is stated is that God made His people male and female, joined together in physical union, become *one* — before Him.

The Pharisees must have wondered about this omission, because they asked why Moses had given rules for divorce. And here Jesus did bring in love. Moses allowed divorce,

He said, because they knew so little of the meaning of love, but God's original principle was that two should become one, inseparably.

By putting the stress on the "oneness" of marriage, Jesus was in effect saying that marriage calls for a certain expression of love. (Here again is the Biblical principle that love is proved to be either true or spurious, *according to what it does*.) In the marriage relationship, love is expressed in faithfulness to one person, just as in the parental relationship, love for our children is expressed in preparing them to leave us and live their own lives. What we frequently think of as love — romance, sexual attraction, or whatever you call it — is really not love at all. It is instinctive, born of our nerves and glands. It may lead to love and enhance love, or it may lead to betrayal of a marriage vow, to an affair.

Older cultures did not consider romance necessary to marriage. Parents arranged marriages for their children on other grounds — suitability or financial or political advantage. The children had to do the best they could, and out of marriage build love.

We now are convinced that love ought to precede marriage, forgetting that romance is based on mystery. And mystery doesn't last. Marriage, and getting to know one's husband or wife, banishes mystery. Some people, equating its going with the loss of love, never go on to the next step, the one our ancestors knew: out of marriage grows love. There ought to be a natural progression — we love, therefore we marry, and because we are married we build a deeper love.

God ordained marriage, and marriage calls for love. Love within this relationship expresses itself on the man's part by being responsible for the wife, by being tender in his care (Ephesians 5:25-33); on the wife's part by helping her husband and by assuming a subordinate role in the relationship (Genesis 2:18, Ephesians 5:24); and on both their parts by being faithful. Paul further tells us that in marriage we no longer have absolute rule over our own bodies but owe a willing submission to our spouse (I Corinthians 7:1-5). That is the Biblical definition of love expressed in marriage. It is the one instance when there is a limitation put upon any expression of love. One man — one woman.

We do, in fact, limit our love in all our relationships. We love our children more than other children, some friends more than others, and some people not at all — but in these *we* set the limitation, not God. It is a good thing to love other children as we love our own, to love more rather than fewer people. Only in the case of sexual love between a man and a woman is there a limit put. That may be why Jesus later said (Matthew 22:30), "For in the resurrection there is no such thing as marrying or being given in marriage — men live like the angels in Heaven." Apparently in heaven there will be no limitations at all upon love, which will eliminate sexuality as being an inadequate expression of love for the completeness we will know in heaven.

Even within the limits of marriage, however, we do not completely possess another person. The Bible says we give ourselves, not that we are given ownership over someone. The one man-one woman relationship in marriage doesn't mean that two people suddenly narrow their universe to themselves, shutting everyone else out. No friendships, no involvement or interest in the rest of the world — how abnormal! To want *all* of your spouse's waking thoughts devoted to you, to resent the friends and the place they occupy in his or her life is possessiveness in its extremest form. It is not love, although it may once have been love before it became warped and sick.

Jealous Love

We have all suffered at some time with an acute case of jealousy; as children, perhaps, sulking because the "best" friend liked someone else; as young men and women living through the dreadful emptiness of unrequited love. Jealousy is the black underside of possessive desire, and it is so purely destructive that we all are forced to recognize its evil. Why do we succumb to it? Why, knowing how it can twist and tear and literally shred the fabric of a relationship, do we tolerate it for a moment? For that matter, why should anyone want to possess another human being so utterly as to shut out all others from the circle of life?

When we sit down and begin to think about these things it becomes apparent that possessiveness and its dark shadow, jealousy, are born out of hatred, not love. First of all, out of self-hatred. All of the possessive, jealous people I have known have been quite positive they were not worth loving. It does seem more than coincidental that these poor unhappy people should all be obsessed with the same idea — their own worthlessness. That is why they must possess completely. In order to be quite, quite sure that their friend or lover *really* cares for them (they secretly cannot believe anyone would love them), they must see it demonstrated twenty-four hours a day. Any interest shown in anyone else, the slightest friendship displayed toward others, is an unbearable threat, confirming their worst suspicions — they are not really lovable, and this new friend or acquaintance will surely supplant them.

Anyone who has been wearied by the insistent demand for reassurance on the part of a friend will know that such possessiveness finally produces the very attitude it fears: irritation followed by boredom and dislike, and in the end, disinterest. Once some years ago I met a young woman in the course of church activities and we became casual friends. At least I thought we did. What she thought became only too apparent each week. We would meet in the usual manner, at some meeting or other and visit for awhile, then move on to others. After I had gotten home came the inevitable phone call: "Eileen, I just couldn't stand it any longer without calling you. Have I offended you in any way? You seemed so cold and distant today, and hardly spent any time with me at all. You know how much I think of you, and I wouldn't want to. . . ." and on and on and on.

The first time she called I was astonished, the second time I was annoyed and after that I avoided her as much as possible. How could one be friends with such a person? I began to feel she had invisible tentacles reaching out to smother me and suck the life out of me. I couldn't break that relationship fast enough.

Then there is the sort of person who is always there. Morning, noon and night this empty soul appears for coffee, sometimes with the apologetic remark, "Well, here's the nuisance again." I'm sure we've all known someone like that, the pathetic creature who always has problems to talk over, who seems so humble and so grateful for your friendship; always apologetic about being such a bother, but nevertheless continuing to insist on your time and attention. After awhile even the most patient person begins to sense that here is no ordinary need, but a sick soul needing special help. Such a person, terribly, desperately in need of love, cannot receive it and often has none to give. Nothing, no amount of attention and concern will be enough for people who are convinced in their inner hearts that they are basically unlovable. All the problems and all the surface troubles stem from this self-hatred.

The obvious answer for such a person is to help them accept the love of God as shown in Christ; but some people are too sick, emotionally or mentally, to find even the love of

God easy to accept. The great lump of self-hatred that lies
at the center of their being will permit nothing else to come
in. Only patient and constant demonstration of the love of
God — lived out in a human life — is adequate for such a
situation. Perhaps the first thing to do is help such a sick
soul find a competent Christian counselor. Having done so,
we can stand beside them, not as a counselor, but as a
friend. It will be difficult and very wearing, because such
people cannot give friendship in return; but all of us, at
some time in our lives, find ourselves so involved, and we
must give what we can.

The Cure For Grasping Love

We've been discussing others — those who impinge on
our lives with their demands for love and acceptance, and
whose demanding and jealous grasp at our attention becomes a problem. But what if that sick person is me? What
do I do about that? I may be destroying my husband by
my resentment of his business friends, or his time spent with
men bowling or fishing or golfing; or even of his service at
church; suspicious of even a friendly hello to a woman. Or
I may be sick inside because I feel that the women who are
my closest friends are shutting me out, they like other people
more than me — I am fearful that they don't really like me,
and afraid there may be something in me that is not like-
able. What do I do then?

The very first thing to do is to accept the fact that
God loves me. He loves me as I am. I don't like the way
I am, but He loves me anyway, even if I don't love myself.
Must I remain this way? Are the things I don't like about
myself things I can't change, like the color of my eyes, or
the size of my ears? Probably not. Then I am free to
change them. But changing myself does not come about by
a concentrated self-study. It comes in only one way, by

one path —a deliberate turning *away* from myself. First to God, and then inevitably to others.

A sense of worthlessness is nourished by constant, unceasing attention. It takes all the time and thought of which a person is capable to be focused on himself for such an unhealthy attitude as self-hate to flourish. The best way to kill the obsession, then, is to begin by removing the attention. When we think about God, that is good. That is the first step away from thinking about ourselves. A better thing is to talk to God. "Oh, well, prayer!" someone always says, as if prayer were something never indulged in unless all else had failed. In reality, prayer is the first thing we turn to because without it all else will surely fail.

The important thing is to be completely honest with God. Most of us know that if there is something wrong, say between two business associates, it must be honestly talked out. No amount of working around or "making up for" an issue will do. It must be faced. What is true in human relationships is true with God. He won't do anything about our problems until we tell Him what they are.

Not that He doesn't know what our problems are, of course. But we must admit our need before He can help. And it is reassuring to realize that, knowing the secrets of our hearts, He is still willing to listen, because He loves.

"Father, You know my heart. You know how much I hate that woman because she's spoiling my friendship with . . ."

"You know I don't want Tom to be on that committee, that Jones girl is so attractive I'm afraid he'll become interested in her . . ."

"You know the terrible joy I felt when I heard that awful story about . . . the meanness, the spite, the malice."

"I am helpless, I can do nothing. I need Your forgiveness and I need Your grace and love in me to change these things. Help me. Do what I can't do for myself." That is the pattern of our asking God to help. There is no point in hiding our sins behind generalities, since He knows them all too well anyway. He can do nothing for us until we ask.

Having done that, the next step is to begin to think about the others in our lives — as themselves, not as little shadows or puppets for our convenience, but as real people. What will help my husband? Or my wife? What do my friends need? Should I make that daily phone call to so-and-so? She's busy, I know, and I'm always haunted by the knowledge that I'm probably a bother. Well, then I'll begin by not phoning her today. What can I do, what can I think about, to keep me from slipping back into that obsessive concern with me and my need for the time and attention of others? Even if it's only scrubbing down the walls, any-thing I do — *anything* — will be constructive, if it breaks the pattern of self-concern.

It doesn't sound easy, does it? It isn't. It's hard, but necessary. Day after day after day it must be done — con-sciously think, deliberately turn the thoughts from the self to God and then, having asked His help, turn to others. If it's too much to handle alone, then by all means run, don't walk, to a good counselor. Far better to talk your troubles out with someone qualified to give real help in the light of the Bible and in the knowledge men have acquired about our mental and emotional makeup than it is to be constantly discussing them with friends. It's true that it helps to share our deepest thoughts with a good friend, but there is a great difference between that mutual sharing which strength-ens the bond between two friends and the incessant chatter about one's own problems that some of us indulge in, and which plunges us deeper into self-concern.

Freedom to Love

All these unpleasant facets of possessiveness we've been discussing — the demand for exclusive affection, the jealousy, the obsession with self — *all* are twisted products of a secret hatred of self. Those who are sure of their acceptance by Christ and at ease in their relationship to others do not need to be possessive. They are free to love, and this freedom is given to us by God. When Jesus said, "If the Son, then, sets you free, you are really free!" He was talking about that ultimate freedom from the slavery of sin which only He can give (John 8:36).

But is it a sin to be sick with self-loathing? It is surely a sign of some inner *malaise* — but a sin? Once we know we are loved and accepted by God, to indulge in morbid self-reproach is wrong. "What God has cleansed let no man call unclean."

On the other hand, there is no room for self-congratulation in the Christian faith, especially since we exhibit, all too often, the same poor imitation of love that the pagan world shows. In the same letter in which the lyrical passage on love (the basis for this book) is found, Paul scolds the Corinthians for being "carnal." Carnality in the scriptural sense simply means human nature untouched by Christ. Our instinctual drives, our emotions, our intellects, all that we are simply on the human level is carnal. Possessive love is carnal. We are told not to be carnal, not to live on the simply human, unredeemed level from which we have been lifted by Christ. "Do not, then, *allow* sin to establish any power over your mortal bodies . . ." wrote Paul to the Roman Christians (6:12).

There is always a choice. The Christian life is never automatic. True, we have had the prison doors opened, as it were, by Christ. But we can walk out into the brightness of His freedom or we can dilly-dally around in the dark. The freedom we are given by Christ is ours when we obey, but without obedience we can live all our lives in as miserable a servitude to slavery as the most hopeless pagan. And there is no worse slavery than to be in bondage to one's own self, to be so tied by secret hatred of ourselves that we must clutch and snatch at others, possess them completely so we'll be able to forget for awhile our own unloveliness.

We *must* choose to obey, then, to get out of the prison of self-hatred. It may mean the most desperate wrenching of our habits of thinking and acting. It probably will, for the habitual attitude of mind we have, whatever it is, is always being deepened. That is why even such a simple change as giving up a daily phone call which we know has been an imposition on a friend can make a cataclysmic difference in life. Most of what we will do in life, is composed of very small bits and pieces; that is why we are so often deceived about the importance of the little things in life. We fail to see that out of those little things a fabric is being woven and that some day that fabric will be strong enough to hold us fast. If we are weaving, out of the minute and fragile threads of daily choices, a commitment and obedience to Christ, the fabric will one day hold us up when everything else in life falls away; but if we have been spinning a co-coon of jealousy and self-absorption around us, it may some day become a coffin.

After all, possessiveness, although we think of it in re-gard to others — "I want her for myself" or, "That's *my* son, you stay out of his life" — is really imprisoning no one but ourselves. The woman who wanted her son's entire life to be centered around her could not keep him by her demands for his time and love, her whining about his inattention, her pouting whenever he spent an evening away from home. He left. Her thoughts, spinning wildly about him — in his relationship to her, of course, always with her, always de-voted to her — were really binding her fast in a mesh of her own making. We think we are drawing others to us when we are only sealing ourselves away in our tight little cocoons.

Possessiveness is a poison. Any love — friendship, sexual

love, parental love — which allows this poison to take root in it will in the end wither away until no love is left — only a monstrous greed to possess even if it means destruction of the lover and the loved. The freedom Christ offers us, and the life He wants to give us is real freedom and real life, for its substance comes from Him and He is the ultimate reality. That is what He meant when He said, "I came to bring them life, and far more life than before."[1]

---

[1]John 10:10.

4. RX

HUMOR

Love ... is neither anxious to impress nor does it cherish inflated ideas of its own importance. — I Corinthians 13:4

When I'm busy in the kitchen it annoys me no end to open a drawer, expecting to find a certain implement, and search in vain for it. I mutter to myself as I hunt around in various drawers and cupboards, and when my daughter is around she's in gales of laughter. I hadn't realized, until she began to tease me about it, that I always say, somewhere in my monologue, "I just don't understand it, I always put it there . . . I just don't understand it. How could such a big thing just disappear? . . . Now who would put a rolling pin *there*? I just don't understand it." It's gotten to be a family joke, as well as the fact that, because I move quickly, I am always bumping into Donna as I rush around getting the meal. She tells me that in the kitchen I'm omnipresent. The sentence, "I just don't understand it," spoken at times of tension, can bring laughter and ease into the situation.

In the same way we laugh about a family tendency to say to anyone who leaves the table during a meal, "While you're up . . ." and then follows a long list of commands. Please bring more butter, I'd like some coffee, close the kitchen window it's cold in here, and so on. This delight in our human quirks adds to our delight in each other. To take one another with deadly seriousness at all times would be most depressing. The fact that we can laugh at each other — and at ourselves — adds to our enjoyment of one another.

When we say that we like a sense of humor in our friends and those we love, it is this kind of humor we mean. Not the ability to tell funny stories so much as the ability to take oneself lightly. The appreciation of our foibles enables us to accept and enjoy the oddities into which we are plunged by our own quirks. Humor adds lightness to life.

The humor which looks at itself with a quizzical eye and says with a laugh, "You are an odd duck, old boy," goes along with a sense of perspective. We see ourselves in the general scheme of things and at times must laugh at our own bumbling antics. And because we see ourselves in this way, we can appreciate and value others.

The Disease of the Inflated Ego

Now, having said all this, what on earth does it have to do with Christian love? Everything, really, for the one thing that will quench any kind of humor entirely and warp one's perspective out of any relationship to reality is an inflated ego. Paul describes this ego negatively when he says it is incompatible with real love, because love "is neither anxious to impress nor does it cherish inflated ideas of its own importance."

There's no doubt about it, "people are funny." But to

be able to say "people are funny" about ourselves is an inoculation against egotism. Pride cannot see anything to laugh about — we are a terribly serious matter. But pride can't get much of a foothold in the man who can laugh at himself.

On the other hand, how can the proud person, absorbed in his own status and greedy for admiration, love anyone else? To love, one must think about someone else and the inflated ego thinks only about itself. There may be an appearance of love, but it is a mirage; it is only the reflection of esteem for one's self which glitters momentarily in response to admiration from someone else. The desire for approval can never be satisfied, so it is imperative for spouse and children and friends to constantly feed this hunger with praise. When the praise and appreciation aren't forthcoming, there are hurt feelings and offended dignity and chilly distance.

The saddest part of this disease — for it is a disease of the spirit — is that the people so afflicted usually end up walled off in loneliness, with no friends, disaffected families and broken relationships. No one can stand to be always pouring out the syrup of adulation. The more we retreat from such people the more desperate becomes their effort to establish themselves as superior, the more frantic their demands for approval; and, in the end, how bitter and resentful they become — because no one can see just how very, very wonderful they are.

In any church these frustrated individuals can be found. No one wants to become involved with them because the strain of such a relationship would be unbearable. One would have to be always in an attitude of admiration, completely artificial.

One woman I used to see occasionally at meetings always cornered someone in a private conversation. It happened to me once and the whole thing — it could not be

properly called a dialogue because I merely listened and
said "Oh" at times — consisted of a series of complaints
against other women, a dreary recital of their shortcomings
and the wrongs they had inflicted on her, and her own
sterling virtues. She didn't want friends; she wanted a
claque which would burst into applause at the proper in-
tervals.

You can see what devastation this sort of attitude can
work in any group if it is indulged in by two or three
people. No one can be the center of attention at all times,
and there lies the trouble. Only one thing causes more resentment on the part of the inflated ego than failure to
admire him, and that is seeing someone else admired.

It is true there are extreme examples of this dreadful
self-importance, like the woman I mentioned. We all know
them, and we all avoid them. We may feel sorry that they
are lonely and embittered — and they always are — but
nevertheless we stay away. At times all of us feel guilty for
not doing something to help such people, remembering
Christ's love for the lost and unlovely, and yet the only
relationship they will tolerate is on their terms. The first
breath of honesty, the first genuine opinion, and the door is
closed. One must listen and applaud, or forego the friendship, because those are the terms.

Several years ago there was just such a person in my
circle of friends. All of us tried very hard to build a genuine
relationship and we all came to grief. The slightest gift
from her was expected to be greeted with ecstatic cries of
thankfulness — not just once but again and again. Her tales
of her own forbearance in the face of great misunderstanding on the part of others must be met with sympathetic
murmurs of understanding, her enemies must become our
enemies. The hint of a difference of opinion was enough to
provoke a storm of anger. "Well! And after all I've done
for you!" followed by phone calls to tell everyone how

shabbily she had been treated. No honesty was possible, because it was not acceptable and eventually she found herself isolated. *No one* can stand that kind of strain very long.

The Universality of the Disease

Why did Paul mention this disagreeable trait in his passage on love? Was it because self-importance is the opposite of genuine love, or because those so blinded by self-esteem are so ever-present that he wanted to warn against them? No, I think he wrote about this because *there is a little of it in all of us.* It is a legitimate part of our humanness to want to be liked — and more, to want to be appreciated. For most of us this is kept in balance by our perspective; we know all too well our own failings and can chuckle at our absurdities. A well-developed sense of humor is invaluable in maintaining this delicate balance.

My husband was a very modest and unassuming man not disposed to pretensions of any sort, and his way of coping with the attempt to impress was to joke about it. Once in a gathering where some men were telling, in that careful offhand manner that self-importance wears, of their eminent backgrounds, he said when he was asked about his family, "Oh, they were the DuPonts of Switzerland — put the holes in the Swiss cheese." Another time in the middle of a discussion of family trees he remarked that he had given up the attempt on his because it had already turned up two remittance men and a horse thief.

The element in life that makes for both improvement and danger is change. We are not like the rocks, fixed forever in the same shape. We are more like plants, growing and becoming — and sometimes, withering. Therein lies our hope — and our peril. We are, whether we know it or not, making numberless choices each day of our lives. These little choices gather momentum and eventually become ma-

jor decisions which alter the course of life. We choose by
our attitudes and our words — and sometimes by our silence
— to become more one thing than another. A slight tendency toward taking one's self too seriously, if not checked,
can eventually balloon into the inflated idea of one's own
importance which Paul warns is incompatible with love. In
the process, all sense of humor is lost. It must die, because
it would at once see the incongruity of our posturing and
pretensions and laugh them out of existence.

As we read the letters to the new churches in the New
Testament we get glimpses of the problems that troubled
them, and they are about the same as ours. Men and women
then were just as prone to self-importance as they are now.
What jockeying for position, jealousy over another's emi-
nence or anxiety to impress on the part of the fledgling
Ephesian Christians may have prompted Paul to write, "Accept life with humility and patience, making allowances
for one another because you love one another" (4:2). The
same spirit breathes through his letter to the Philippians,
possibly the church closest to his heart:

> Now if your experience of Christ's encouragement and
> love means anything to you, if you have known something
> of the fellowship of his Spirit, and all that it means in
> kindness and deep sympathy, do make my best hopes for
> you come true! Live together in harmony, live together in
> love, as though you had only one mind and one spirit
> between you. Never act from motives of rivalry or per-
> sonal vanity, but in humility think more of each other than
> you do of yourselves (2:1-4).

Paul had never yet visited the church at Rome when
he advised them:

> Let us have no imitation Christian love. Let us have a
> genuine break with evil and a real devotion to good. Let us

have real warm affection for one another as between brothers, and a willingness to let the other man have the credit
(12:9, 10).

No doubt he had in mind, as he dictated those words, the
difficulties and problems of the little churches he had helped
to found and knew so well, and he was sure the church at
Rome would be very much the same.

Some attitudes seem to be harder to put up with on a
personal level than in a group. It is often possible to work
quite satisfactorily on a committee with many whose idio-
syncrasies make a closer relationship undesirable. But this
particular attitude — being anxious to impress and having
very inflated ideas of one's importance — is at its worst in
a group. You see, we can simply stay away from these people as individuals, but in a group their grim determination
to be on top of the heap makes them troublesome to the nth
degree. There they are, in the middle of everything, their
ruthless pursuit of status leaving destruction in its wake.
What can we do about it?

First of all we can remember that they are our Christian brothers, whether we are overjoyed about it or not. At
the very least they deserve as much consideration as the
most hardened pagan — and that's quite a lot. The pattern
for us to follow in our relationship with those outside the
faith is the one Jesus gave us:

> Love your enemies, and pray for those who persecute you,
> so that you may be sons of your Heavenly Father. For he
> makes his sun rise upon evil men as well as good, and he
> sends his rain upon honest and dishonest men alike (Mat-
> thew 5:44, 45).

The trouble is, it's really far easier to be magnanimous
toward a disagreeable non-Christian (we even get a spiritual
"kick" out of our forbearance) than it is to show the same

tolerance toward another Christian. "What kind of Christianity is that?" we mutter indignantly. "He ought to *know* how wrong he is. Can't he see how pushy and obnoxious his behavior is?" And all the time, underneath our honest and righteous indignation lurks the self-congratulatory thought, "Thank goodness *I'm* not like that, always putting myself forward and trying to grab the spotlight." In a way it might be said that one of the worst things about the inflated ego is that it acts as an irritant which always sets up a reaction in others — a counter sin to match its own dark color.

We are all deeply affected by this. Either we are, as vastly inflated and pushy egotists, constantly setting up waves of irritation around us, or we are being irritated. Yes, there is enough of the "pusher" in us to be frightfully annoyed when it gets out of control in anyone else. *The thing we dislike in others is quite often the thing we can't stand in ourselves,* even if we know it's tightly controlled. Just to know it's there at all is galling. How very easy it is to look with dislike and judgment at the very trait in someone else which we cannot bear in ourselves!

There are some failings we don't mind admitting — quite serious ones, at times — but not this one. To admit that one is anxious to impress, or has grandiose ideas of one's own importance, is to admit that there is no basis in fact for such an attitude. It is an admission of inferiority, of lack, and to face *that* requires the very humility which the inflated ego does not have.

How to Be Proud Though Humble

Up to this point we have been discussing oversize self-esteem only in terms of human relationships. But what about God? How can the egotist ever come to know Christ at all, since any relationship with Him is predicated on our coming as sinners needing His grace? Was that perhaps the reason why Jesus began the Sermon on the Mount by saying, "How happy are the humble-minded, for the kingdom of Heaven is theirs"? It looks as though no real relationship with either God or man is possible to the person with an inflated ego simply because he fills his whole universe to the exclusion of everyone else. Others are seen only as blurred figures, for his gaze, firmly fixed on himself, has become spiritually astigmatic and gives a distorted picture of everything.

I can almost hear some perceptive reader mumbling, "Then how did the Church come to have so many of these blimps within its fellowship? Are you saying they're not Christian at all? For egotists they certainly are, and a nuisance and a trouble to get along with!" No, not that they are not Christians. It may be quite possible that some of us, in our desperate need to be "appreciated" were, for a moment, vulnerable enough for God to get through to us with His love. But the attitudes and habitual set of mind of a lifetime do not usually vanish overnight. After the initial shock of actually admitting our need of a Saviour, some of us have reverted to the old stance — this time with a spiritual slant, however. We can say we are sinners, like parrots repeat phrases, but the truth of the statement never registers; inwardly we feel quite sure that we are among God's prize specimens — in fact, that our very "humility" in admitting our sinfulness is ample proof of a truly admirable spirituality.

I don't think I had any real knowledge of my own sinfulness until long after I had become a Christian. Only in the light of God's holiness did my shabby condition become apparent, and for me it took time. My smugness and complacency had to go. But it is the humble-minded of whom Christ speaks in the Sermon on the Mount who are able to respond with the unself-consciousness of children to Christ. They do not (as I did) have to have the veneer of pride and pretense and self-justification and anxiety to be well thought of peeled away before they can see their need. They know their need.

This probably accounts for the bite in the retort Jesus made to the Pharisees who had criticized Him for eating with tax-collectors and sinners (Matthew 9:12, 13). He said, "It is not the fit and flourishing who need the doctor, but those who are ill! Suppose you go away and learn what this means: 'I desire mercy and not sacrifice.' In any case I did not come to invite the 'righteous' but 'sinners.' "

The attitude of the Pharisees toward anyone who did not devote himself to keeping the minutiae of the law, as they did, was one of condemnation. The uneducated and poor were damned, they said, because obviously they did not know the law and so could not keep it properly. That hardness toward everyone outside their little sect had blinded them to their own needs. Jesus' quote from the Old Testament was a thrust at the very heart of their self-satisfaction — *they* were the ones who made the sacrifices, who were in the Temple morning and night. But they were also the ones who showed no mercy to others. Then with a devastating sarcasm He told them He had not come to call the righteous, but sinners.

Knowing their Scriptures as they did, the words He did not speak aloud were almost audible as He faced them: "There is none righteous, no, not one!" They knew what He meant. He meant that we are all in the same pickle barrel: the obnoxious egotist so full of self-importance that he thinks God fortunate to have him on his side, and the "spiritual" Christian, who, critical of the egotist, deludes himself that there is none of that in him.

Yes, the Church is full of Christians who are still in bondage to their own overweening pride, who are self-important and pushy and jealous of their prerogatives. Some of us have only a taint of this in us, and some of us are so filled with it there is room for nothing else, but the remedy for all of us is the same. Christ alone can heal the disease.

Restoration of Perspective

I said awhile back that the person so afflicted never really "sees" anyone else, since his vision is blurred by the inflated image of himself which distorts everything around him. The discipline which can begin the cure of this awful sickness is the practice of thinking about others. By that I mean serious thinking, not just a lazy movement of the mind, for a second, toward those faceless "others" before reverting to absorption with oneself. I mean thinking about people one by one. The best place to start is when we pray.

When you pray for your husband, for example, really think about him. What does he want out of life? If you don't know, your relationship has been alarmingly unbalanced. Is he just the man you think God appointed to get you everything you desire, or is he the man you were given to as a helpmeet? What troubles him? (Most of us would far rather pray about the things in him that trouble *us* than about what troubles him.) Is he tired, is he discouraged, is he constantly stretched too thin?

Or your wife. You snap at her when the business day has been difficult. Have you ever thought about what this does to her? Or is she just the dim figure there at home to be snapped at? When she complains do you really listen, or do you let the tide of irritation rise in you so that you shut her off in a way you wouldn't dare use on a difficult employee? You'll have to practice this discipline doggedly; it isn't easy. When we have hardly bothered to think about others except as they make us happy or unhappy it's hard going to think of them suddenly with all the dimensions of reality. We are much more comfortable regarding them as flat figures which will fold up like paper dolls when we are through with them.

Some parents never really *see* their children as human beings, but as extensions of the ego, or as accessories to enhance their own lives. It is, "My son, who is doing so well at the University," or, "My daughter, such a sweet girl — she's never given us a moment's trouble." We are so hurt and angry when they become rebellious, or when they get into trouble, or refuse to conform to our standards, because it reflects on us. Our delicate egos are wounded. This is natural and inevitable, I know. We want to be proud of our children, to see them make the right choices, become worthwhile adults. There is a difference, however, between longing for them to grow into solid, well-balanced Christians, and pushing them into competition for honors so as to feed our own pride.

No one wants to be used. We all know, instinctively, that if we are not of value *just as a person* no accomplishment will be enough. We want to be seen, not in our function, or capacity, however we excel in it, but as *I*, a living soul worth loving. Because of this deep need, we are invariably offended by someone whose own self-esteem blinds him to us. We do not like to be merely "the audience," part of a mass. Therefore the antagonism aroused by a truly self-important person instantly makes the recognition he needs impossible.

Children see things very clearly, and sometimes instinctively react to this egotism on the part of parents. Their way of expressing frustration and hurt at being used as an extension of the parent-ego is to damage that ego by striking out. Does Mother want me to be a good boy? I'll be the worst boy in the neighborhood then — I'll *make* her really look at me, even if it's only in anger. Am I being pushed at school and into all kinds of activities at which I am supposed to excel so my parents can brag about me? I'll fix it so they'll be hurt the way they've hurt me.

That's the way it goes. Again, the only cure is for parents to *see* their children as real, live human beings with souls of their own, who will make their own choices (not always what we wish they would), live with their own mistakes, have their own experience with Christ (not necessarily the same as ours). Just as each one of us is responsible before God for our own lives, we are not responsible for anyone else. We may be called to account for our faithful adherence to and presentation of the truth as we know it (and the words, "as we know it" imply the fragmentary and relative nature of our knowledge of truth). But that is all. Since we cannot answer to God for our husbands or wives or children, we must accept them as responsible beings. The freedom to become a person includes the freedom to make choices.

Children must learn this discipline of seeing too. How many eager young converts have gone home and "witnessed" to their non-Christian parents with the most praiseworthy zeal, while continuing to live the same grubby, whining, selfish and self-centered lives they always lived? A minute's thought would lead them to see that what was needed was not sanctimonious preaching, but some sanctified living — a sweeter attitude at home, responsibilities assumed without grumbling, an end to the quarrelsome bouts with brothers and sisters.

Day by day we must continue to practice "seeing" others. As we do, the astigmatism in our vision will vanish with the reduction of our own inflated image. It just isn't possible to remain smug and self-satisfied if we put our attention and thoughts on others, because we are what we think.

Prescription — Laugh at Yourself

If, at times, we find ourselves cross because somehow in a group the conversation never seems to lead around to the point where we can tell about our daughter's accomplishments, or the eminent friend we've acquired, that's the time for a little humor. The inflated ego never laughs at itself. It can't, for that would destroy its pretensions. Laughter is the best weapon to turn on ourselves when this temptation arises. We may have to forfeit the admiration we hoped to elicit, but that's small loss. Admiration and love are not always compatible? We *admire* achievement, but we *love* a person — not because of what he's done, *but for himself*.

The proud person laughs at others, never at himself, because to laugh at himself would destroy his self-image. Usually he reacts with furious anger to any humor directed at him. Think of all the instances of Jesus' humor — never slapstick, often pointed and satirical — which sent the Pharisees stomping off in a rage. He told a story about the ridiculous excuses men made to avoid a dinner engagement to point up our silliness in rejecting God's call, and the legalists got the point. They didn't see the humor, they saw only that it described them and they didn't like it.

I have found that when I react negatively toward one of Jesus' parables, it's time for careful self-examination — there's a sore spot that needs dealing with. Once I have admitted my need to God and accepted His help, I am relieved of the necessity of pretense. I can even laugh at myself — an infinitely small human, posturing and pretending before the limitless expanse of the universe. Humor gets me into proper perspective again.

5. ALWAYS

IN

STYLE

Love has good manners and does not pursue selfish advantage.
— I Corinthians 13:5

When I was a little girl, my mother used a switch off our apricot tree on my legs if I was naughty. I must have been a slow learner, because I have *very* vivid memories of the sting of the switch on my legs. Actually my parents were not abnormally strict, but even so there was an impressive list of things I knew I would be switched for: "sassing back," for instance; pinching, hitting, kicking, pushing, when I was very small. Later the list changed: disobedience, lying, "being smarty," unkindness to my friends (someone always tattled) or not doing my allotted household "jobs."

It was years later that I saw what had been going on in my life during those early years. I was learning that failure to obey — and obeying always entailed assuming some responsibility — brought swift punishment. No one ever sat down and systematically explained to me why good manners, or courtesy, was important, but the sometimes painful process of growing up, prodding tentatively at the fabric of manners to find a hole and being promptly punished, gave me a healthy respect for minding the rules. I sulked and pouted at times, and I remember giving way to bouts of self-pity in which I made long speeches to myself about the unjust requirements of the adult world of "manners."

Not being enlightened moderns, neither my mother nor my father would have dreamed of laboriously explaining the "why's" of the rules to me, and I probably wouldn't have understood if they had. How could a child of four be expected to understand that she causes the grownups in a room to be extremely uncomfortable when she comes screaming into their midst with a demand for instant attention? Children see themselves in the center of their universe and really *cannot* understand that other people are as important as they are. That particular truth is acquired slowly and spasmodically as they grow up.

"I Know Just How You Feel"

One of the most electrifying experiences of my young life was the time when, in the second grade, I came upon a new girl in the room, sobbing bitterly into her coat in the cloakroom. When I asked her what was the matter she said with the simplicity of anguish, "I am the only one who has to wear knee socks!" I was struck by an unfamiliar emotion — for an instant of time I entered into her life, and shared her feelings of being new and lonely and, worst of all, looking different from the others. If I'd been ten years older, the only thing that would have served would have been the cliché, "I know just how you feel."

And that is what manners is all about — "I know just how you feel." Love, the love which has been transformed and brightened by the grace of God, has good manners because it "knows how you feel." Between that knowledge and the sometimes reluctant obedience of the four-year-old stretched years of minding the rules and a growing understanding of their meaning. I didn't wake up one morning to a flash of insight — "Ah, at last I see the point, good manners are necessary because if we love people we want to make them comfortable." But little by little, sometimes in sudden glimpses of the truth but more in a growing awareness of others, the point of courtesy became apparent.

I think that is how most of us learn about that aspect of love — just by growing into it. Once my daughter came home from Junior High school with hurt feelings written all over her face. She was the monitor in her seventh grade sewing class, and when the end of the period came she was supposed to tell the girls to put away their sewing things. One girl, on being told it was time to clean up, slapped Donna's face and told her to shut her mouth. (Needless to say, the teacher was out of the room.) Donna, who had never been slapped before, was too surprised and shocked to do more than stand there. Her comment when she had finished telling me about it was, "But you know, Mother, she wears awful clothes and she smokes after school on the sidewalk, and I guess she just hasn't been brought up right." She knew that good manners are acquired, not innate, and was beginning to see that they are part of the fabric of love.

Good manners are not synonymous with the accepted behavior of any particular group, not even of the very sophisticated. For those cultic patterns of conversation and attitudes may at times be the very opposite of good manners, designed only to make everyone outside the group feel very *un*comfortable. The underlying reason for courtesy, or gentility, or any of the synonymns for good manners, grows out of love; genuine love is concerned that others be put at their ease. Even such a common thing as table manners stems from this sort of concern; those with delicate stomachs will certainly be nauseated by the sight of a man hunched over his plate like a vulture, chomping and dribbling his food, and making noises like an animal.

When Jesus said, "Treat other people exactly as you would like to be treated by them — this is the essence of all true religion," He was talking about honesty and kindness and fairness. In all of these, good manners is an essential ingredient. Implicit in the courtesy we extend to others is the acknowledgment that they are *worth* consideration. A lack of courtesy is an insult because it carries with it the implication that the person so treated isn't worthy of anything better.

Genuine Love Has Style

The point of Paul's statement, "Love has good manners and does not pursue selfish advantage," is that *genuine love has style*. It is not graceless or awkward. It dispenses its kindness and good deeds and helpfulness with a delicate sensitivity for the feelings of others. Without style the most generous behavior can be offensive.

Style, according to the dictionary, is the following things: "A particular, distinctive, or characteristic mode of action; a mode of deportment or behavior; one's bearing or demeanor." It is also a mode of fashion or living. I use it, as I think Paul would, to mean that our characteristic mode of action, our behavior, ought to conform to the style of Jesus Christ. He showed great sensitivity to people's needs. So should we. He had compassion for their frailties, concern for their ills, graciousness in His dealings with them.

Jesus' graciousness, His style, was innate. Like the maxim that a gentleman behaves like one because he *is* one, Jesus was gracious because He was grace. We don't have His style, His grace, naturally. We have to grow into it, and at times behave with graciousness we don't feel. Obedience to God always brings the reward, and the "feeling" will come. We will be letting His style become our own.

Could it be that a great many earnest Christians, anxious to excel in Christian witnessing and the good works Jesus commanded us to do, offend because of their lack of style? I think so. There are thousands of men and women, as well as high school and college age people, products of the evangelical Christian world but now in rebellion against it. When one talks to them for any length of time it becomes apparent that what they are really revolting against is not so much the Christian faith as the total lack of style, the appalling bad manners displayed by a large part of this world.

Let me give some examples. One woman I used to know, whenever we talked together, always got around to giving me all kinds of good advice, larded generously with Bible verses. I'm sure if I told her I was having trouble keeping my grocery bill down I got some spiritual advice on that, with an appropriate quotation from the Bible. She never seemed to have problems herself, and invariably ended the conversation with something like this: "Now, my dear, just pray about this and I'm sure the Lord will show you the way. I'm go glad we've had this little talk, because I always say that no matter how tired I am, I'm never too tired to help someone." I felt like a peon being given largesse by the bountiful lady, and I didn't like feeling that way so the friendship cooled. *She had no style.*

I was told recently by a young woman about her experience in a Sunday school discussion group of young married people. They were talking about witnessing. One

man said, "When I'm out with business friends and I am
offered a drink, I always say, 'No thank you, *I* don't drink
because I'm a Christian' "! *That's* bad manners. That's
rudeness, and insensitivity and a dreadful inability to imagine how others feel. How do you suppose those around
him, having their drinks, felt when he said that? Sorry because they, too, were not so pious? No, indeed! They felt
they had been told, in a backhanded way, that their tee-
totalling associate was better than they were and wanted
them to know it.

One zealous Christian leader, a youth worker, used to
conduct testimony meetings at conferences. He would frequently interrupt the testimony of some young man or
woman to correct their theology, instruct them in what they
should have said, or quiz them sternly on some point in the
talk. To see the flushed, embarrassed faces of those hapless
young people was a source of acute discomfort to me, and
I'm sure to others. We could sense the humiliation, the feeling of being publicly chastened on the part of these un-
fortunate ones. That man had no sensitivity toward others
at all — no manners — *no style.*

No one wants to feel like an object of charity, and all
too many Christians succeed only in making the rest of the
world feel just like that — as if we Christians simply are
using them as straw figures to practice our spirituality on.
The suspicion that we are not really concerned with them
as *people* is often confirmed by the truly dreadful manners
we exhibit at public meetings. The perfunctory greeting,
the professional smile which is sometimes only a stretching
of the lips, the glazed stare which never really "sees" anyone
but leaders and special friends.

A group of us were discussing this disagreeable lack
of manners among Christians one evening, and one young
man told about taking a friend of his — a girl about twenty
— to an evening discussion group for college-age people.

He knew she was not a Christian, that her life lacked direction, and that she was eager to find friends. The very first person they encountered when they entered the room was an extremely personable young man, one of the "leaders" of the group, often seen on the platform making announcements or praying. The girl was introduced to him, and he said, as his eyes slid past her to someone he knew, "Oh, yes, awfully glad you could come, Miss — er . . ." and walked past without another word. The young woman turned to her friend and said, "So that's a sample of Christian fellowship, huh? *Thanks* a lot!" She turned and left, and that, so far as I know, has been her last contact with the Church.

I've heard Christians talk about the "offense of the Cross," and recount touching tales of the misunderstanding they have endured from "the world" because of it. Frankly, I don't believe it. I think the world is offended by our offensive manners, not by the Gospel which they probably haven't heard because we are so graceless, so hard, so isolated in our pious withdrawal from what we consider to be the contamination of "the world." Jesus never was like that. He was criticized by the Pharisees, the most religious people of the day, for His association with all the wrong, common people. These common people wouldn't have responded to Jesus in the wholehearted way they did if He hadn't obviously enjoyed them. It may be this characteristic which annoyed the Pharisees above all else. They made their contempt for everyone outside their sect painfully obvious. One may witness to these poor unfortunates, but one must on no account *like* them. They must be made to feel that they are pretty grubby objects, and it is very good of us to take notice of them at all. If they repent, they may, of course, enter the kingdom of heaven, but should always maintain a respectful distance from us, their superiors, here on earth.

Bad manners, or lack of "style" in the Christian world, has nothing to do with protocol, or an acquired set of social customs, nor indeed with any kind of polish, or veneer. It is simply lack of love, or a love that lacks; a love so poor, so shriveled, so faint that there isn't much of the grace of God in it. The grace of God is just that — *grace*, a quality which, like style, seasons everything with a genuine regard for the reactions and feelings of others. I think it's far more urgent for Christians to consider their manners than it is to engage in soul searching about their success (or lack of it) in witnessing, or their "spiritual" lives (dreadful phrase), or any number of drives and campaigns to "get" more people. Good manners would instantly see the falseness in the phrase, *"get* more into the church." We *get* things; we *know* people. There is no other way to bring people into the kingdom of God than by knowing them and letting them into our lives, and so drawing them. That takes good manners.

Love Has No "Ins" and "Outs"

It may at first have seemed odd that Paul coupled having good manners with another phrase, "does not pursue selfish advantage," but surely by now it has become apparent that the two belong together. Using people for our own ends, as objects to practice witnessing on, or doing good to them so we can tell about it in a testimony, is pursuing a selfish advantage — and bad manners. It has no concern for them at all. One of the things I dislike most is to feel used, and I suspect that a great many recipients of our Christian largesse feel used. No wonder they stay outside. It's warmer there.

Like everything else in the world, all that is good and true and real in manners has an imitation — its counterpoint in the realm of shadows. We all know that every group has tended to develop its own style, its own language or slang,

its own distinctive image. You can see this displayed with
unconscious humor any time a group of teen-agers is observed. They have their own language. It gives them a
feeling of security, of belonging, to be able to walk down
the street talking loudly in a special jargon to each other, as
if unconscious of passers-by listening in, but the very loud-
ness betrays the fact that a great deal of the fun of being set
apart in such a group lies in using the special slang where
others — the outsiders — can hear. The fun of being "in" is
at its height in the presence of those who are "out."

Unfortunately, this juvenile emotion persists and is often
hardiest in Christian circles. It is inevitable that we have a
technical, specialized language when we are talking theology; like any other science, theology produces its own technical terms. But need we use that sanctimonious "slang" in
the presence of those to whom it means nothing? It doesn't
enlighten them, and it does make them feel their position as
outsiders acutely. Could it possibly make them want to be
"in," to be able to use the slang? I doubt it. The terms we
bandy about usually impress non-Christians as archaic, and
it may be that they are right. It is certain that the early
Christians spoke to their world in terms it understood. If
we want to have any communication with our world, we'd
better do the same. Or do we get a secret thrill of egotism
when we carelessly speak, in the hearing of our non-Christian friends, of those who are "under conviction," those whom
we have "witnessed to" or, worst of all, "led to the Lord"?
Do the terms, "being right with the Lord," or, "sharing
what's on my heart," or any of a dozen other clichés have
any meaning at all for them? Indeed, some of our language
is so incomprehensible to the average modern man that his
emotions on being exposed to it are akin to those he feels
when first reading the instructions on the 1040 Income Tax
Form: utter bewilderment!

I have just come from church, before writing these

words, my feelings ruffled and hurt — not deeply, just
scratched a little in my sensibilities. I was speaking to two
young men, both graduates a month or so ago of one of our
seminaries; I am very fond of both of them. I made some
comment, a trivial one — perhaps even a stupid one. Their
response was immediately to laugh, look meaningfully at
each other, raise their eyebrows and generally behave as if
they had been entertained or offended or both by an idiot
child. I felt humiliated and hurt. Evidently what I had
said was not worthy of anything other than contempt. I
mention this because it's symtomatic of something I've been
aware of for years — that acquiring knowledge about the
Christian faith, as students in seminaries do, often goes along
with losing all sense of courtesy toward others. They hardly
make an effort to conceal their great superiority, and it is
impossible to carry on a conversation with one of them without being continually corrected, lectured, or — worst of all —
tolerated kindly.

To be sure, this kind of rudeness is not limited to
seminarians. There are certain social groups within every
church which have their own jargon, their own "code," and
whose conversation is so sprinkled with references to mysterious happenings and people known only to them that to
be in their presence is to be consumed with misery. It is
hard for me to believe that those who indulge in this are
totally unaware of the effect they have on the "outsiders."
Producing such an effect is part of the fun — the fun of being
"in." I know that all of us are guilty at times of making the
newcomers to a group feel out of it. But usually it is without
intent, a thoughtlessness which is bad enough. What really
bothers me is that so often the rudeness seems to be pro-
duced on purpose, and since the result is to make the person
on the receiving end thoroughly unhappy, the purpose has
to be malice. When we commit this sin — it is a real sin,
though without even the dignity of desperation, only petty,

demeaning and cruel — we are offending God as much as if
it were He on whom we turned our mockery.

Why do you suppose Jesus used so many parables about
farming and fishing, the earth and plants and trades and
daily tasks of life in His teaching? Was it because everyone
who heard Him knew exactly what He was talking about?
Very well then, we must do the same thing. We must con-
front each other — and the world around us — in terms we
and it understand. We must do others the courtesy of speaking their language, as Jesus spoke to His contemporaries.

The technical language can be saved for the times when
we are only with others who know how to use it as we do.
It is a kind of "family" language, saved for intimate occasions. And what is true of our language is true of everything
else in our lives. Our manners, to be truly loving, must
create an atmosphere of warmth, of absence of strain, of
relaxation. We do *not* have to compromise our Christian
faith to be courteous.

Love Meets People Where They Are

The first thing we might do, in meeting others in this
spirit of gentility and courtesy, is to cultivate a genuine
interest in them and what they are doing. I use the word
"cultivate" purposely, because we will have to work at it; it
doesn't come naturally. We have been so accustomed to
thinking of ourselves as having he best possible life in terms
of our church services, our meetings, our Bible study groups,
our parties, all of which we must reveal to a waiting world,
that it may take a bit of doing to adjust our thinking to *their*
point of view. They probably do not think they need church,
or meetings, or Bible study, and their real needs are not
going to be paraded for the clinical interest of a casual
Christian.

Fortunately most of us, unless we are totally walled off

from reality, live and move and work in the same world non-Christians do. And *there* is our point of interest. Business problems can be intelligently discussed, the price of groceries, international affairs, the news of the day — this is where we meet our world. The troubles that plague us all are real troubles, not shadows, and need real sympathy and concern. I once heard a Bible teacher say to a friend who had been telling her of a non-Christian's trials with her husband, "Forget the problems with the husband, get her saved, that's the real problem!" True, of course. But human beings are so constituted that we cannot talk to them about ultimate issues until we have shown our genuine concern for them as real, three-dimensional people by taking seriously the immediate issues that need to be solved. There is only one recorded instance in the gospels in which Jesus spoke directly to a man's spiritual need before He considered the physical need. That was when He healed the paralytic whose friends had ingeniously lowered him through a hole in the roof. At that time He talked to the man about his sins, and told him they were forgiven. Then He gave the word of physical healing. Again and again, however, we find instances where it says simply, "and Jesus healed them . . ." or, "proclaiming the gospel of the kingdom, and healing all kinds of illness and disability."

In discussing Jesus' healing ministry I am not primarily interested in the question of healing, but simply using His response to their need as an instance of the genuine love of God. This love takes people seriously, listens to their problems, considers their needs. *In short, it does them the courtesy of meeting them where they are.* No doubt Jesus saw the spiritual misery of the hordes who crowded around Him as the true horror, but He met them just as they were, on the level of their understanding, and healed their bodies and their minds.

There is no stronger demonstration of the love of God

than this, that He stoops, in His grace, to meet us in a way that we can understand. For some of us it may be half a lifetime before He gets us to the place where we see that our only real need is for Him — not for His blessings.

What would have been the response if Jesus had said to the waiting wretches, "Now, my good people, you think your physical illnesses need healing, but actually what you really need is spiritual healing. Never mind how you feel, just get right with God and it won't seem half so bad"? Do you think for one minute that a cripple who had spent his life in bitter envy of those who walked straight and whose waking hours were obsessed by his wretched condition would believe in a love which dismissed that condition as of no importance? Of course not.

The principle Jesus used was that of going straight to the need that was uppermost in a man's heart and meeting that need. When that happened, men's hearts were melted and they thought, "Why, this man cares for me — really cares!" Then, like the man born blind, they could say, "If this man did not come from God, He couldn't do such a thing!"

That is the pattern laid down for us to follow — the good manners which meets each man and woman as a person, which listens and responds to a person, which does all it can to make a person feel at ease. This kind of good manners stems from a love which says to itself, on meeting someone, "I wonder how she feels and how I can help her be comfortable," not, "I wonder if she has noticed how well turned out I am and how much attention is paid to me by all the really important people in the group?" Some Christians dispense cordiality as if they were royalty being kind to the common people. One can observe them dropping this distant graciousness immediately when they speak to someone they know and like — or someone more "important" than they. *That's* not good manners, that's "pursuing selfish advantage" — being nice to someone who can give status by his friendship.

Developing Style

Good manners, far from being a superficial and even rather worldly quality, are an essential part of genuine love. Since we are born into the Christian life as we were into the physical world, we will grow in love just as we grow physically. The love that starts as a very small thing in each of us, a tiny spot touched and brought to life by Christ, grows as it is cultivated. One of the ways we cultivate it is by practicing good manners.

Some people are immediately suspicious that once we begin to "do" anything at all, in the sense of practicing an action or cultivating an attitude, we are trying to work up a kind of legalistic righteousness. I think this idea, a sadly warped one, may be responsible for a great deal of sloppy Christian living. Everyone just expects to become automatically spiritual, so no attention at all is paid to the one thing Jesus said was essential. He said it both at the beginning and the end of His earthly ministry:

> It is not everyone who keeps saying to me 'Lord, Lord' who will enter the kingdom of Heaven, but the man who actually does my Heavenly Father's will. . . . Everyone then who hears these words of mine and *puts them into practice* is like a sensible man who builds his house on the rock . . . (Matthew 7:21, 24)

Three years later He said, "If you keep my commandments you will live in my love."

Just a fragment, that last sentence, out of His discourse in John 15, which begins with an illustration of Jesus as the vine and His people as the branches. Any good we do will be the result of His life in us, we know, as the illustration showed. But we are living souls with the power of decision, not plants which simply exist but do not decide whether or not to bear fruit. Therefore to use this illustration to show that we "just naturally" will be fruitful when we are in Christ is to twist its meaning.

We do decide! A thousand times each day we decide — to get up or to stay in bed; to speak pleasantly before morning coffee or to snarl; to snap back when someone is cross or to refrain; to smile or not to smile; to say yes or to say no. Limitless possibilities of action flit through our minds, and out of these we elect to choose one. This is our part, and God will not do it for us. Call it obedience, call it response, call it what you will, but it involves deciding and then doing our part.

That simple, inescapable responsibility is the constant factor in all aspects of our Christian lives, and the deciding factor in whether we will grow as Christians or not. Growth comes as we obey. In the very first chapter of this book we discussed Jesus' words to the Pharisees, "If anyone wants to *do* God's will he will *know* . . ." The words might be paraphrased, "he will *grow*. . . ." And that is important for our present concern with good manners, the courtesy of the Christian life. Manners, not being something we are born with either physically or spiritually, are acquired by growing into them as it were.

The method is simple. By obeying what we know to be Jesus' command for today (attention to studies in school, good work on the job, getting the work done at home, treating difficult Mrs. X with kindness), we are doing several things. We are growing into the spiritual habits of obedience and decision; we are doing the particular thing Jesus intended for us to do at this time; we are learning the good manners He teaches; and we are keeping ourselves open to Him for further teaching. If it sounds too simple, remember that it is just the way we expect our children to grow in everything they do — and it works the same way.

Style, as the dictionary says, is "a particular, distinctive, or characteristic mode of action . . . deportment or behavior; one's bearing or demeanor." That is what Paul was talking about when he wrote to the Christians at Rome:

> Don't let the world around you squeeze you into its own mold, but let God remold your minds from within, so that you may prove *in practice* that the plan of God for you is good, meets all his demands and moves toward the goal of true maturity (12:2).

Our lives are to conform to *God's* style, and we are told that although it is not always easy, in the end we will find it has become our own.

6. DOIN'

WHAT COMES

NATURALLY

Love ... is not touchy.   — I Corinthians 13:15

"Love . . . is not irritable or resentful."

At this point I can imagine someone saying, "This is too much! A description of love which rules out all human fallibility, all faults of temperament and personality — this is ridiculous! After all, you can't change human nature. We know our weaknesses, but no one expects perfection of us and we must just make allowances for each other." That is an admirable sentiment, and the Bible tells us to do just that: "accept life with humility and patience, making allowances for one another because you love one another" (Ephesians 4:1).

However, before we simply throw out this description as being far too idealistic for us (what *can* the writer have meant, since this is obviously unreasonable?) there are two things that ought to be said.

All of us find it impossible to get along in life with any degree of harmony without making allowances. Touchiness (or as the Revised Standard Version has it, irritation and resentment), however, is the very thing which does *not* make allowances for others. The absence of tolerance and understanding is the very essence of irritability, which doesn't flourish where there is forbearance for others. We might say that where there is a vacuum — the absence of tolerance — nature, which abhors a vacuum, rushes in with irritation and touchiness. And that brings us to the second thing that needs to be considered.

Irritation and resentment and touchiness are natural. We do not have to learn them. They are "just there." They are like unbrushed teeth, unwashed bodies, tangled hair, dirty houses. They are there when we do not go to a great deal of trouble to alter them.

"Back to Nature"

A great many people say we should shrug off our painfully acquired culture and simply "be natural." By this they mean, do just as our instincts move us, without the controls of training and discipline. They paint a picture, all in the most glowing colors, of a wonderful life in which we eat, make love, fight, sleep, just as animals do, without inhibiting our "natural" instincts in any way. The idea sounds marvelous, especially when one is tempted to do something forbidden by morals or convention. Back to the simple uncluttered world of nature! How glorious!

Only it isn't.

The very ones who are so eager to do away with troublesome restraints as far as our relations with each other are concerned do not suggest throwing off the rest of civilization's advantages — the baths, the deodorants, the toothbrushes. They do not advocate that we should cook our food in pots over open fires or give up refrigeration. Not at all! They like everything about our culture except the restraints it places on their relationships with other people. In a way it is as if they said, "I want to be an adult because there are so many privileges only an adult can have. But you must expect no more of me than you would of a child because I intend to keep those privileges too."

Paul's discussion on love has something to say to this notion. "Natural" love, like all natural instincts — hunger, a love of finery, fear, a desire to scratch — is, left to itself, doomed to die. It will wear out with the weariness of age, or be nibbled away by inevitable irritations and frustrations, but it will not last. It is part of us as our digestion is part of us, and that digestion is destined for dust.

The life we get when we give ourselves to Christ is not an extension of natural life, which ends in the grave, but an entirely new thing — life in another dimension, untouched by death. Death may be an incident, but it is only an incident in this new life. The quality of it, the eternity of it, belong to Christ. It is His, His eternal life which He gives us — a conferred thing, something which He adds to our lives. We do not have it naturally. Left to ourselves we grow old and die, and all our natural loves and hates with us. The life that lifts us out of that cycle of aging and death is a supernatural thing added or given when we are *in Christ*. It is not as if He just patted each one of us on the head and said, "There now, I've given you a new kind of life. Run along now and do the best you can with it." The words, *in Christ*, mean that in a far deeper sense than the word "literally" conveys, we are lifted out of the old, natural life, and are taken into His.

That new life in us touches and transforms all our natural instincts. Not diminishing them, nor crushing them out to make us poor sticks with no more vitality than robots, but transforming them — in a sense doing to them what we do with our children. We begin when they are first born to teach them to acquire a love of cleanliness and of manners. Left to themselves they would stay dirty. Left to themselves they would behave like animals, kicking and biting and scratching when displeased. Great pains are taken to train them to subdue their natural inclination toward animal behavior and to learn to enjoy being clean and polite and educated.

Did you notice the words "learn," "teach," "train" relating to the process we all go through in order to grow up? Growing up doesn't just happen; we have to be taught by someone else. The romanticists, who belive in the untrammeled natural life, unrestrained by artificially learned manners and morals, would like to drop all that and go back to babyhood, as it were, and start again doing what comes naturally. *But only* in one area — that of human relations. They like the comforts of an artificially acquired civilization as well as the rest of us.

Such people are fond of accusing Christians of being totally artificial; Christianity may say, it isn't natural. Rules, guidelines for living, prohibitions are something added, something foreign to natural man, and therefore Christianity is false. Only that which is "naturally" there is real.

At a certain stage of life this reasoning can sound very persuasive, but I think a moment's consideration shows its weakness. The argument is illogical, for one thing, and the actuality is not really desirable, for another. The talk about just "being natural" means behaving as if there were no culture, no modes of behavior, but at the same time behaving that way surrounded by all the advantages of culture. These advantages would disappear in one generation if everyone suddenly took to behaving "just naturally," because it is *not* natural to work to improve our environment, it is not natural to build roads and bridges and cities and study medicine, or indeed to study anything. Natural living is animal living, in a den or a cave. All of civilization is highly unnatural, in that sense.

The whole concept of going *back* to nature is illogical because it talks as if doing or adding anything to nature — in this case to human nature — makes it *less* than it would have been if left alone. Think about that for a minute. Do you feel less of a person because you know how to read and write, because you have learned how to think logically, because you have a knowledge of history and the arts, perhaps of economics? Of course not. These acquired things have made you *more* of a person, not less. They have increased your understanding of the world you live in and of yourself. To go back to the natural state would be to divest yourself of all that has made you what you are — and who wants to be a baby again?

The romanticist might say that he really didn't mean that at all. Of course it's all right to have knowledge, but let us simply be more natural in our pursuit of pleasure, in our enjoyment of love. Let us not be deprived of the joys of life because of the rigidity of rules which confine and inhibit.

A good case could be made out for the idea that this point of view admits only a partial view even of nature. It is a part of our nature as human beings to want to improve things as they are — in every realm. When the romanticist rhapsodizes "nature" he does so with a mental reservation which blocks out man's natural desire to "tidy up" nature.

Natural Reactions

It won't work. We are all of a piece. The discipline that gives bounds to our indulgence of ourselves in the moral realm is the same discipline we draw upon in every other area. We are inclined to divide ourselves up into tidy little compartments; one for business, one for family, one for friendships and so on. And if the compartment we have for personal relationships is set aside for special indulgence, we think it won't affect the others. But it does. The areas overlap.

In the realm of human relationships there are two things that happen "just naturally." One is to be absolutely unrestricted in taking what we want — highly touted by the romanticists as free and untrammelled love. The other is to react with irritation and resentment, or touchiness, when we are prodded by any kind of annoyance. Life on that level is about what animals in a cage have: the sight of food makes them drool; pat them and they wag their tails; jab them and they snarl.

The connection between uninhibited morals and an uncontrollable temper seems remote, but it isn't. They are two instances of the same thing — animal reaction, born of the nerves and the glands. They share other similarities: discipline in both areas is anathema, and both betray an utter absorption with the self. One says, "I'll set my affections on anyone I happen to want regardless of other people involved"; the other says, "I'll explode if I want to and snarl if I want to because I don't care how anyone else feels."

Since these two attitudes toward life are so compatible — one attitude, really, expressed in two areas — one would think that those who hold to either of them would be extremely understanding and tolerant of each other; but quite the reverse is true. We find men and women whose lives are lived without the remotest bow toward morals demanding that those around them treat them with all the thoughtfulness and self-restraint that only a close attention to courtesy can give. This is also true of those who are touchy and easily offended — real grouches. They often have no sympathy for anyone whose moral codes are more elastic than theirs might be. Of the two, the touchy person is harder to live with, though that is not to say that excessive irritation is a worse sin than immorality. The man or woman who goes heedlessly through life without the least regard for his morals, or those of anyone he wants to possess, can certainly do a lot of damage. The results are usually heartbreak and guilt and tension and trouble for a few lives. However, the disagreeable person who vents his bad temper on anyone who gets in his way does just about as much damage — though perhaps less traumatic, less earth-shaking. He just makes everybody around him a little bit miserable all the time. Of course, if he's a member of your family, perhaps a lifetime of such misery is as wearing to the system as living with a philanderer.

Immorality and Love

In any book or article on love most people's minds jump immediately to sex. Surely, they think, there will be some purple paragraphs about the heinousness of unchastity, a whole chapter devoted to the necessity of keeping oneself pure before marriage, and so on. When we read the Scriptures seriously on the subject, however, we find that the most famous passage on sexual immorality — I Corinthians 5 and 6 — discusses the issue without one single reference to love! As a matter of fact, sex is seen rather as a matter of appetite. This pains some sensitive Christians, but that may be because we have developed an odd delicacy in many areas where the Bible is quite frank. The Bible talks as if love and passion were not always the same thing; sometimes they go together, sometimes not. Passion, like any other appetite, can be indulged in lawfully or unlawfully, and the boundaries are clearly defined.

Love, on the other hand, is depicted in many different ways, and always it is shown in action; the entire passage used as the basis for this book is simply a description of love in action.

There are two reasons, I think, why Christians, along with the rest of the modern world, have tended to confuse love and sex. The first is that we have so glamorized and sentimentalized the sexual side of romantic love that we have come to think that sex is all there is to it. When we talk about love, it must be sex we mean. The second reason results from this confusion. We read all the passages on love (they are as thickly sprinkled through the New Testament as the punctuation) without ever seriously taking them to heart. We slide easily over the words, "Let us have no imitation Christian love," as though it were telling us merely to be as pleasant as possible. Often we whisper a kind of inner refrain under our breaths as we read, a refrain reducing all the clarity of love's actions into a blurred, out-of-focus snapshot of fairly inoffensive living.

The Biblical image of love is one of attitudes as well as actions. Most actions stem out of attitudes. An attitude is a permanent set of the mind — toward goodness, for instance, or respect for the rights of others. A fleeting emotion may make it difficult to act according to our real attitude, and that is why we excuse such lapses by saying, "I know I shouldn't have reacted that way, but I was so tired . . ." We know that we have betrayed our real attitude by letting a mere feeling overcome us. Paragraph follows paragraph in the New Testament about the attitudes of love, building up a picture of love transformed — and informed — by the love of God. Courtesy is an attitude as well as action. Touchiness is an attitude. Possessiveness is an attitude. Patience is an attitude. Pride is an attitude.

Why so much emphasis throughout the whole of the New Testament on "little things" like attitudes rather than on "big things" like adultery or sex perversion? Many of us would far rather — and often do — burst into impassioned speech on the evils of today's morality than on the virtues of brotherly love. Why is this?

The Double Standard

Could it be because we are so adept at evading the issue? Like Adam and Eve in the garden we are busy hiding our real nakedness — which is spiritual poverty before God. We are always erecting a spurious morality in order to conceal our inward immorality — not the obvious kind of pagan immorality, *but the deeper immorality of self-centeredness and pride and impatience and irritation.* When Paul, as in the 13th chapter of I Corinthians, talks about these sins of attitude, we say, "Don't look at me — look at those immoral people with their loose morals — *that's* sin!"

As far as I can tell, sin is sin and the Bible condemns it all equally. The social sins wreak devastation in life which must be lived with. God's forgiveness does not do away with the consequences of sin. *But* so much more is said in the New Testament about the sins of attitude — pride, greed, envy, malice, deceitfulness, spite — than about the social sins, that there must be a reason. I think God knows our fatal tendency to point the finger of scorn at those whose sins are plain to see in order to remove attention from our own cherished little sins. We don't even call them sins. We call them "besetting sins," by which we usually mean that since we do them so much they surely can't be too bad; or we excuse them by a thousand devious pleasant evasions. They are "weaknesses," or "my kind of temperament," or even, as one disagreeable woman once said, "my honesty"!

The Bible talks about "small" sins of attitude so much because we tolerate them so readily. It is unfortunately true that in the Christian world the social sins are really believed by many people to be far more sinful than the sins of attitude. Those who have commtited some gross sin may be admitted to the bosom of the Church but they are expected to walk softly, to carry about with them a sort of invisible

aura of penitence. They are, in short, second class citizens
of heaven to many Christians. The New Testament does not
bear this out. For instance, Paul, to the Galatian Christians
gave two lists: the first, all the evils that stem from our
lower or unredeemed nature; the second, the qualities the
Holy Spirit produces in us (5:19-23). In the first list the
sins of the flesh and those of the spirit are jumbled together
with no distinction made as to whether some are worse than
others.

> . . . sexual immorality, impurity of mind, sensuality, worship
> of false gods, witchcraft, hatred, quarreling, jealousy, bad
> temper, rivalry, factions, party spirit, envy, drunkenness,
> orgies and things like that.

You'll notice that quarreling, jealousy, bad temper
(touchiness), rivalry, factions, and party spirit are listed
along with the worst carnal sins. But, if we are to be honest,
we must admit that we have allowed them to exist — sometimes even flourish — within the family of God. *Yet we are
not horrified at their presence.* That is the worst of it.

We are, in a sense, adopting the point of view of the
romanticists who urge us to "go back to nature" to live a
fulfilled life, except that they mean we should "be natural"
only in the area of physical urges while we permit it only
in the area of temperament. All the excuses, the rationaliza-
tion or explaining away which we do to justify our tolerance of the sins of temperament (irritation, resentment,
touchiness) and all the things provoked by those sins (that
horrid list of Paul's) cannot change one thing. And that is
that the Bible regards them very seriously indeed.

Our toleration of this double standard of measuring
sins — one for the obvious sins of the flesh, the other for the
sins of the spirit — is the biggest reason that the non-Christian world thinks us to be hypocrites. They see, very clearly,
our smug acceptance of the sins of attitude and tempera-

ment, our pretense that these things aren't really bad, worst of all that we often justify them in the name of Christian righteousness — a piece of sophistry which rightly earns the contempt of the world. We talk about the love of God and they laugh at us because they see so little of it in our lives.

Love Transformed

Paul wrote, "Love . . . is not touchy." When Christ comes into the human heart He brings His grace to transform our natural love, sometimes poor and shriveled and easily quenched, into His perfect love. His love is not touchy, is not irritable or resentful, and will not be diminished, however feeble our response may be. These characteristics He came to give to us. If we remain just as we were, sensitive and easily put off, easily angered or irritated, onlookers may rightly suspect our relationship to Christ to be quite superficial. We need to turn immediately to Him for forgiveness and renewal which may be necessary countless times each day — but we must do it. There is no limit to His forgiveness (He expects even us to forgive "seventy times seven"), and no alteration in His love for us. All we need to do is ask.

No doubt progress will be slow, but if there is anything genuine in our commitment to Christ it will come. The "natural" life we have always had, along with animals and fish and insects, will be gradually infused with something new. The spiritual life could well be described as that which doesn't come naturally. When it does come it does not simply negate all that is natural; it transforms it, makes it deeper and richer. It is not too much to say that it gives us a foretaste of the glories of heaven, when what we now call the "spiritual life," haltingly learned, will become truly "natural."

7. " ... TO
FORGET,
DIVINE "

Love ... does not keep account of evil or gloat over the wickedness of other people. On the contrary, it is glad with all good men when truth prevails. — I Corinthians 13:6

It has always been easy to love some people. Sometimes we love them for selfish reasons — my Dad always gives me anything I ask for — Mother knows just what I like — she's my best friend because she always understands and sympathizes with my troubles. Sometimes we are fascinated by charm, or beauty, or sheer magnetism, or an indefinable something that evokes love. But then, the world has always been like that. Whether you read contemporary novels or the mannered stories of Jane Austen or the romance literature of medieval Europe, *love is seen as something that happens to us.*

Love is our response to another person, called forth by something in that one, and we could no more help it or hinder it than we could, by willing it, stop our bodies from getting hungry or sleepy. It just comes. People who have complicated their own and others' lives by falling in love with the wrong person usually say, "I just couldn't help it."

This universal notion that love happens to us like the measles or a sneeze or a yawn is responsible for the equally universal idea that love is its own excuse for anything we do. Marriages broken, families split, lives wrenched out of order — all these things are too bad but necessary because "I just couldn't help it."

When Paul tells us not to keep account of evil or gloat over other people's wickedness, he is saying that we *can* help it," that we are responsible for love. This is not merely a command to abstain from negative attitudes, it is a command to be positive.

Love Is For Enemies

Up to this point we have agreed with Paul's correctives. We can see how much better it is to be patient than impatient, how helpful to be constructive. And although it is hard to do, we can see that our love ought to be free of possessiveness. Since we dislike pride so in others we agree we ought to avoid conceit and self-importance ourselves. The necessity of good manners is fairly obvious, and all of us respond to the ideal of loving selflessly, hard as we find it to do. And to love without irritation or touchiness is attractive. We are shown these things and everything within us agrees that they are good, that however far we are from achieving them, we can give ourselves to the process of becoming more loving.

But, for a good many of us, we can see ourselves as being more loving in this way only in relationship with people we would naturally love anyhow.

We can see that our natural loves, subject to fits of irritation and selfishness and sulking if we are taken for granted, need to be infused with God's grace. And yet, since the idea of love as a sort of involuntary response to lovableness in someone else is so persistent, the idea of love for disagreeable people, people who have wronged us or slighted us or deliberately shut us out of their lives, is hard to accept.

How hard a time we all have when we read Jesus' words, "Love your enemies, and pray for those who persecute you, so that you may be sons of your Heavenly Father. For he makes his sun rise upon evil men as well as good, and he sends his rain upon honest and dishonest men alike" (Matthew 5:44, 45). We even tend to have a sort of contemptuous tolerance for those who try to practice this. "He's spineless," we say, or, "Oh, he's the sort of man who won't take a stand on anything." The attempts to explain what Jesus meant in terms more acceptable to our human frailties are numerous and perennial. Too frequently we rationalize His words to make them apply only to a future life, hoping to avoid their implications for us here and now. "This is a picture of the ideal community," we say, "the community of Heaven, not of earth." Or we say that we *should* strive to achieve this difficult standard, but of course we know we won't come near it. Or else we throw the whole business into the back cupboard of our minds and go on to something more "practical."

Forgiveness Is For Friends

At first the words, "It does not keep account of evil or gloat over the wickedness of other people," seem to refer to our attitude toward those we do not naturally love — our enemies. In most of us there is a natural — not nice, but natural — inclination to feel a triumphant satisfaction when someone we don't like is seen to be blameable. The secret none of us will admit if we can help it is that *everyone* — even those we love "just naturally" — becomes unlovely to us if they irritate or annoy. The hard command to love our enemies, to do good to those who despitefully use us, has to be followed at times among friends and even in our own families.

Human love without the transforming power of Christ in us is all too ready to pile up dreary statistics of misdeeds which we hold against even those we love the most. Oh, we don't call it "keeping account." We call it "hurt feelings" or "righteous indignation" or any one of a number of things. But what it really means is that our love curdles when it is offended.

Lovers' quarrels, tension and coldness in marriage, estrangement between parents and children often come as a result of our tendency to cherish grievances. No human relationship can endure for long without a great deal of forbearance, or making allowance, or putting up with — and as we have seen, the New Testament is full of advice to do that. But that is not enough for the kind of positive, vital life God has planned for us. In another place Paul said that we were to be "always ready to forgive if you have a difference with anyone. Forgive as freely as the Lord has forgiven you" (Colossians 3:13).

What we are doing when we file away the slights, hurts and grievances we have suffered is to refuse to forgive. We may say we have forgiven, but as long as we remember and, at each new quarrel or disagreement, trot out the old complaint, we have not forgiven at all.

I speak on this subject with real authority because all my life I have been prone to remember — yes, to cherish remembering — harsh words, words spoken in anger, all the myriad offenses we daily suffer (and daily commit, although we seldom remember *those*). There came to be certain sensitive areas in my marriage, as I suspect there are in most marriages. Past misunderstandings and unhappy arguments were piled up under the surface of life and each time the tender spot was touched they were all dragged out for a depressing review. My husband used to say I had the memory of an elephant: I could remember every word spoken in all the years of our marriage.

It was a long, long process of learning and suffering the results of my own reluctance to forgive before I began to catch a glimmer of the liberation there is in forgiveness. You see, *it is only ourselves we cripple when we refuse to forgive.* We may hurt others, may by our attitude make them unhappy for a time, but an unforgiving spirit is a boomerang that turns back and deals the deadly blow to the one who sent it.

All sorts of unpleasant things occur on the human level when we keep account of other people's sins and failures; we are walled off from each other by our own hardness. It is impossible to have any kind of genuine communication between two people when one is holding the other off behind a shield of resentment. And we all know how miserable we can make ourselves by this hard, prickly, unforgiving spirit. It warps and twists our vision until we are finally unable to see others clearly as they really are but only as our bitterness has painted them. No love, no warmth, can penetrate that defensive barrier.

Forgiveness Cancels Justice

The thing that makes it so difficult to be sincerely loving and forgiving when we have been injured — or think we have been — is that there is just enough justice in our position to delude us into thinking ourselves *entirely* justified. It *is* wrong to gossip, wrong for a husband or wife to say unkind things about the other in public, wrong for a friend to break an engagement because someone more important asked her to do something. When one has been "gossiped against," or has a genuine grievance against a friend, that strong sense of justice, of fairness, which we all have within us, rushes to protest the indignity.

That this innate respect for justice or fair play is present in everyone (though much stronger in some than in others) is evidenced by the pains we all take to justify our own actions and our embarrassment when we cannot. It is the "eye for an eye, tooth for a tooth" philosophy, and it is universally understood. We appeal to this sense of fair play when we say to a naughty child, "How would you like it if someone pinched you the way you pinched Johnny?"

But the whole of our Christian lives is founded not on justice but on mercy. If God held us strictly to account for our misdeeds not even the most righteous person would pass muster. The first thing we learn on becoming a Christian is that our acceptance by God depends upon His grace. He accepts us, not because we are so nice, but because He loves us and sent His Son to do for us what we could not do for ourselves. The cross is the symbol of God's judgment upon sin as well as of His mercy in taking that judgment upon Himself in the person of Christian.

The second thing we learn is that, having entered a new life by way of the cross (His kind of life), we cannot now live the old tit-for-tat life (by which we were actually condemned according to the same standard we used to judge others). We are to begin becoming like Christ. I say "begin becoming" because obviously it is a process of growing and won't happen overnight. And in this new life the single greatest thing that will be required of us is that we forgive. No more keeping account of wrongs done us, for our own have been forgiven.

Peter spoke for all of us when he asked Jesus how many times it would be necessary to forgive someone who had wronged him — perhaps as many as seven? Jesus gave God's answer when He said that seventy times seven was more like it, and then illustrated it by the story of a man who, having been forgiven his inability to pay a tremendous debt to his employer, went out and threw a fellow servant into jail for a debt of a few dollars. The master, on hearing of this, sent for the servant and said, " 'Didn't I cancel all that debt when you begged me to do so? Oughtn't you to have taken pity on your fellow servant as I, your master, took pity on you?' " Jesus finished by saying that the man was thrown into jail until he could pay the whole debt. "This is how my Heavenly Father will treat you," He added, "unless you each forgive your brother from your heart" (Matthew 18:21-35).

It isn't that God is capricious or ungenerous toward us, waiting to see whether or not we'll treat others with compassion before He extends forgiveness to us; it is that we *already*, having been accepted by Him through Christ, have had our debt canceled. Our acceptance of our new standing as free, forgiven children of God, is validated by a new spirit of forgiveness toward others. If we are still using the old system of bookkeeping in our relationship with others, then in our hearts we have never really received God's forgiveness. Not that He hasn't given it — but we haven't taken it, for if the channel is open, it will be open all the way, not closed at one end.

I suppose Jesus used a ridiculous example to make His point, the first debt being so enormous — thousands of dollars — and the second one being so small. But then our debt to God is ridiculously large, and our grievances against each other, in comparison, are just as ridiculously small. It all seems so plain when it is pictured that graphically. How is it that we have such a hard time forgiving?

Forgiveness Frees

For me (how it may be with you I cannot say), it has been an uphill battle partly because I was very slow in learning to take God seriously. I think our initial acceptance of His forgiveness has to be ratified daily — sometimes hourly. And I had been a Christian for a long time before I even *began* to catch a glimpse of the enormity of the debt God could have held against me. Daily struggles with the same old temptations, the same besetting sins were dreadfully humiliating. Rather than face it, as one must when one prays, I would have done any number of disagreeable tasks. Do something nice for the Lord — anything, anything but be forced to say, "Here I am again, Lord, with the very same sins I had yesterday."

That reluctance to keep the channel clear with God has another side — it shows itself in an unforgiving attitude toward others. A great breakthrough in my life came when I had been hurt and humiliated deeply by a friend. The experience was so shattering that I was upset over it for weeks. Finally I came to the place of desperation, because I knew I had to be able to forgive freely in order to have any peace in my own life. I prayed. Prayed every day — and the minute I got up from my knees, the same old resentment rushed back. I kept on praying.

It was not easy — but then, not many people are so difficult and stubborn as I am — and months went by. Since my friend was not in the same city I could go a long time without the old resentment and hurt, but of course that was because I hardly ever thought of her. I must admit that when she came to mind, my first emotion was one of remembered anger. I had to pray some more.

Finally one day she came to visit, and suddenly — the moment I opened my door — the anger, the hurt, the resentment had gone. I felt light and free. What had happened? God had been busy. As I prayed to be able to forgive, He brought to my mind some of the dark spots in my own past — unkind words conveniently forgotten, petty deceptions, neglected responsibilities, quite an appalling list of misdeeds. These were things God had not "kept account of" but had freely forgiven. As I remembered, somehow my friend's offense against me kept shrinking until at last it disappeared.

Really, what God was doing was getting me back into the perspective of seeing things His way instead of from the old, he-hit-me-so-I'll-hit-him point of view.

One would think that this new kind of life, a life channeling God's grace toward us through to others, would be easy to live with those we love the most, but unfortunately that is not so. We can pass over slights from people we hardly care about on the same shallow level as the acquaintance. But when someone we love wounds us, the thrust goes much deeper and is harder to forgive. That is why nothing less than a constant remembering of God's love toward us will do. Only against such a vast portrait of love can our own little loves be seen in proportion, and our forgiveness seen for what it is: costly to us, but as nothing in the light of the cost of the Cross to God.

There is one great, wonderful discovery which comes with the relaxation of our judgment on others — *they* are freed, just as we are freed. By that I mean that nothing makes one so defensive as the uncomfortable feeling that he is being weighed and measured and found wanting by another human being. It tends to stiffen all the muscles of the spirit. But when that barrage of unspoken criticism is lifted, the defenses go down.

Forgiveness Forgets

One of my dear friends, Opal Hughes, has always been a warm, loving, and charitable woman. She is the sort of person who makes people feel liked and accepted. You know how some people are so nice to have around because they have the knack of making everyone comfortable? Opal does this, not just physically, but spiritually. I have always known that our friendship could be as deep and strong as it is because she has been forgiving toward me. I asked her one day what she found to be most helpful in being free of resentment and the desire to "get even." She said, "I always ask God to help me not only to forgive, but to forget, as if the thing had never been." And that is exactly what God does for us, as He said long ago through the prophet Isaiah: "I, even I, am he that blotteth out thy transgressions for mine own sake, and will not remember thy sins" (43:25). Perhaps an essential part of forgiving *is* forgetting. The offense is wiped out, as if it had never been.

It can be seen immediately that this is terribly costly to the one who is doing the forgiving. In a way, it is a kind of dying — to give up, forever, all our "rights," all the prerogatives of innocence and guiltlessness, and to say, "Whatever has passed between us is gone, never to be called to mind, never even hinted at in conversation or demeanor; but really and in fact, gone."

We must even forgive when the person who has injured us never seems aware of what he has done nor of our generosity in forgiving! To be hurt deeply and then forgive is hard enough. But to have it taken lightly — that is expecting more than human nature is capable of! But we must.

At once, if we are called upon to forgive to this extent, we are seized by an immense reluctance to give up any part of our righteousness. For the fallen human ego there is nothing so satisfying as dwelling upon wrongs done to ourselves. All the delights of martyrdom, the pleasure (we hate to admit it, but it is) of describing to sympathetic friends the outrageous behavior displayed by others, and the wicked joy in drawing, by contrast, our own sinlessness. Yes, if we are honest we must admit that there is something of this in each of us. It is only human. But human nature is spoiled by sin.

On the other hand, to forgive so utterly, so completely as to blot the thing out, is going to extract a very high price, and from the one who has been already hurt. Words hastily or carelessly spoken can never be unsaid, steps once taken leave indelible prints. But then, as we said before, whatever we may have to pay in generous forgetting, in overlooking past misdeeds, in accepting without recrimination is microscopically small seen through the lens of God's forgiveness, and forgetting, of our sins. That is our only safe measuring stick — not our own generosity, dwelt upon and lovingly cherished until it cancels out our forgiving, but His generosity, His unclouded acceptance of us. Anything less than this is not genuine forgiveness; and nothing could be worse than having to put up with the spurious version of forgiving offered by some Christians.

Some years ago I knew a woman who was always forgiving people, but with her it was a kind of vice. She would say to someone who had wronged her, however unintentionally, "That's all right, dear, I have already forgiven you. As I prayed about it this morning it just came to me that no matter how much I suffer, it is really for Him, and I am willing to forgive. I always think God gives us these trials so that we might show forth His grace." As if that were not bad enough, the incident would be referred to innumerable times in casual but unmistakeable terms, always in the presence of a number of people and always in terms that left the meaning plain. One had to suffer being forgiven over and over and over again, and publicly. That woman had the fun of having it both ways. She could congratulate herself on her spirituality, her Christian forbearance in forgiving, while at the same time enjoying all the forbidden pleasures of exposing her victim's misdeeds; and all of it cloaked in a most nauseating Christian sweetness. Remember, Paul said, "Let us have no imitation Christian love."

There is no way out of it, forgiving is hard — and costly. But pretending to forgive, while slyly dragging the offense out for public view, is worse than an honest grudge. Helmut Thielicke in *The Waiting Father* comments on the spiritual pride that lies behind this sort of imitation love: "Thus the devil again succeeds in laying his cuckoo eggs in a pious nest."

Now we begin to see how far from sentimentality the Christian Gospel of love is. We have talked, written and preached so often about God's love and forgiveness, without giving them content, that we have come to accept that glossy, shallow version as the reality. The measure of God's love and forgiveness is the Cross. The Cross is also the measure, the sum total, of human evil and sorrow. All the bitter words, the lies, the whispered slanders, the heartless laughter, the silence that rejects — the Cross is the price God paid for our share of that guilt. Yet all is summed up in the words of God, spoken through Isaiah, when He declares, "I, even I, am he that blotteth out thy transgressions for mine own sake, and will not remember thy sins."

Many of us have a very hard time imagining how this could be. How could God literally "forget" our sins? We have known too well the spurious forgiveness that all too often passes for the real thing; the martyred air as we are graciously pardoned, the constant little reminders of our culpability, the easy suspicion with which we have been regarded. Many a husband, having once betrayed his wife and repented bitterly does not dare to be fifteen minutes late from work. His wife *may* have forgiven (which I doubt), but she has not forgotten, and will never let him forget.

It seems to me that an essential part of forgiveness, then, is the forgetting. Unless a thing is truly gone, dropped into the void of forgotten things, it tempts the one who has been sinned against to dredge it up again. I know this is not always possible on the human level. Sins which radically alter the course of life carry their own reminder with them in their results. In this sense the Cross is the permanent reminder of all our sins as well as the sign of God's forgiveness. Also, we do everything imperfectly, but that is no reason to give up trying. We are told to be perfect as our

Father in heaven is perfect, which implies that we are to be unalterably "set" toward following His commands, including the difficult one to forgive seventy times seven. No doubt there will be many failures, but the important thing is that we keep on obeying as best we can.

"I can't do it," you say, "it's not human to be able to forget such a thing." We are not told to be human; we are already that, we need no instructions in doing just what comes naturally. The Bible is full of exhortations to be more than human — to let Christ do *in us* something supernatural, which only He can do. If we find it impossible to understand just how Christ can so change our inner lives, our real selves, as to make such forgiveness and forgetting possible, let us remember that we can't *really* understand God at all, how He could love us, how He could die for us, how He could possibly forget our sins. We do not really grasp, although we try very hard, any more than the very edges of most of the doctrines of the Bible. The Trinity, the two natures of Christ, these things can be somewhat imperfectly defined but never completely comprehended. So it is with the way God works in us. We do not need to understand nearly so much as we need to obey.

Forgiveness Is Commanded

Obedience has such a large part in the teaching of the New Testament for two reasons. One, because it is where we always begin with anything; *we obey, then we know.* Secondly, because although it is the first essential, it is so contrary to our nature. Obedience in the matter of learning to forgive and forget means that we practice by doing. We practice forgetting the sins done against us, just as we practice remembering our own obligations toward God. Since psychologists tell us that we forget things we really don't want to remember — like dentist appointments, and so on —

we can make it easier to practice forgetting by concentrating on the good things in life rather than the trying episodes.

It is probably no coincidence that Paul, in the closing paragraphs of Philippians, spoke of such an emphasis on the positive. He begged two women, Euodias and Syntyche, to make up their differences — to forgive and forget. Then he gave some practical advice on having an attitude of thankfulness and trust toward God, and ended by saying, "Here is a last piece of advice. If you believe in goodness and if you value the approval of God, fix your minds on whatever is true and honorable and just and pure and lovely and praiseworthy." Instead of thinking of the irritating habits of those who annoy us, which makes it almost impossible to forgive them, we are to cultivate a habit of thinking about things that are true and good and praiseworthy.

Some people are so afraid of "works" that they have come, without quite realizing it, to a philosophy of Christian passivity, as if whatever we think and all our actions must come automatically. The Bible maintains a perfectly balanced tension between these two extremes. It says that we are to work our very hardest to obey all the directions for living that the Bible gives — but always remembering that it is God who is working in us. Paul's writings are full of practical instructions on Christian living, but these are always balanced by a reminder that such a quality of life is not inherently ours — it is added.

> No one can pride himself upon earning the love of God. The fact is that what we are we owe to the hand of God upon us. For we are his workmanship, created in Christ Jesus *to do those good deeds which God planned for us to do* (Ephesians 2:8-10, italics added).

A careful reading of all of Paul's (letters) leads to the conclusion that he was very much aware of our predilection for plunging into extremes, a little as if we had a passion for flinging ourselves off the road into the ditch on either side. Those of us who are on guard against the ditch of "dead works," are likely to back off the road into the ditch of passivity on the other side.

In a sense, the whole of the Christian life (including forgiving) is works. But not dead works. In the Bible, works that are "dead," works that have no life in them, are things we do to try and curry favor with God, as if we could cancel the "counts" against us by an equal number of meritorious activities. That will not do. We are all so hopelessly in arrears that only by God's taking upon Himself, in Christ, our weight of sin and making the payment we could never make, can the debt be cancelled.

And that is where some Christians stop in their thinking. Christ died for our sins, works are useless, so let's praise the Lord and turn on the TV. Don't suggest that we *do* anything — haven't you heard that Christ has done it all?

But has He? One does everything for babies because they are helpless, but we are not meant to remain babies. True, the life in us is a new kind of life, a given thing, Christ's own life; we could never have earned it, it is ours by virtue of His offer and our acceptance. That life, however, like the life that is in a baby, must grow — and everyone must do his own growing, even while fully aware that not only the life within us, but the power to grow, comes from God. The *one thing* God will never do for us — either to bring us to Himself or afterwards in the growing process — is to make up our minds. He has done us the honor of waiting, as a gentleman waits, for us to say, "Yes."

Every single thing that takes place in the life of a Christian, in his growing process, has two parts to it: God, through His Holy Spirit working within us, suggesting, reproving, correcting, sometimes worrying; and our *actively assenting*.

And that means not only accepting God's directions, *but acting on them*. Since forgiving is always hard, we excuse our reluctance to forgive. The very pain involved proves to some of us that our forgiveness is not real. Our emotions remain the same, therefore it must be a legalistic fiction. We find it hard to believe what we do not feel.

We must accept the fact that the whole Christian life is opposed to our natural bent and consists of works — living works issuing out of our relationship with Christ. We will be giving assent to Christ's commands to do things and cultivating attitudes that were, in our natural state, impossible. On our own we could never achieve them. In fact, we will never use the word "achieve," since we will be conscious of a new force at work within us enabling us to forgive — to forget — to love. We will be aware that everything is done by our own volitional act of will, but that the power behind it is not ours but Another's.

Forgiving originates in the will, not the emotions. Forgiving, like any other activity of the Christian life, requires our willingness to practice it, to confess our failures and try again, to keep at it and at it and at it, everlastingly. No one ever said it would be easy. The Cross was not "easy."

Forgiveness Is Creative

We have seen that our forgiveness must include those we love, who can at times hurt us most deeply; those we don't really like very well; and those who have really injured us. They are all likely to be people with whom we have some quite natural relationship. They are relatives, friends, people we know casually in the neighborhood, at the P.T.A., in church, or business associates. The statement that love does not "gloat over the wickedness of other people," however, seems to imply that this forgiveness includes even the opponents of God.

I do not think that Paul meant for us to close our eyes to wrong, pretending that it isn't there or isn't really so bad.

Wrong is wrong, and you can't be for right without being in opposition to wrong. What the phrase means is, I think, that we are to be sorry that evil exists. We are not to allow ourselves the pleasure of being vindictive. And it is a pleasure sometimes to feel vindictive — possibly what the hymn writer meant when he said, "For Thee all the pleasures of sin I resign."

We are at all times a little like dogs, bristling at strangers. We tend to dislike those whose culture is different from ours or whose standards are different (although they may be just as good). They are not what we are, therefore they are suspect. And when it comes to individuals or groups who offend our sense of propriety, or piety, or justice, we are inclined to feel that they ought to suffer for their misdeeds. Our feelings may stem from a sense of justice, but the trouble is they usually slide over the real vindictiveness very quickly. This is true especially if, for instance, someone who is behaving very shabbily and getting away with it is also a person whose wealth or personality or popularity we envy. "Serve him right if the whole thing blows up! Who does he think he is, flinging that inherited money around? Wonder how he'd manage if he had to work for a living like the rest of us?"

And when the whole thing *does* blow up, how pleasurable the warm tide of triumph that wells up within! "Wonder how he likes that? All his money won't do him much good now!" All very natural, but not Christian — not God's way.

But how can we forgive people whose sins have not been against us personally? One cannot really forgive apart from a personal relationship. The people whose wickednesses we are tempted to gloat over might include the Communists, criminals, the opposing political party, people we only read about in the papers. Their sins have been against God and society generally, not against us.

It seems to me that the forgiveness we are called on to have for these people is a symbolic one. We can pray for them. Praying for people whom we may never meet and never know the outcome of their lives is a kind of forgiveness. We know that God honors prayer, that in ways beyond our fathoming our prayers fit into His cosmic plan.

When we practice this kind of creative forgiving in our prayers, who knows what may come of it? One thing, certainly. We will be "glad with all good men when truth prevails."

8. YESTERDAY,
TODAY,
FOREVER

*Love knows no limit to its endurance, no end to its trust, no
fading of its hope; it can outlast anything. It is, in fact, the
one thing that still stands when all else has fallen.*
— I Corinthians 13:7, 8

Love Endures

The word "endurance" brings before my mind an image
of someone rather grimly "just hanging on." It implies things
to be endured. We enjoy pleasant situations, we endure unpleasant ones. Endurance may be very necessary to life; we
can imagine all kinds of situations in which it is called for.
But what connection can it possibly have with love?

Can the word used here simply mean "to last"? In the
dictionary that is the final definition given the word "endure."
Its primary meanings have to do with sticking through something grimly: "To hold out against; sustain without impair-
ment or yielding; undergo or suffer; also, to bear without
resistance or with patience; tolerate. To hold out; support

adverse force or influence of any kind; suffer without yielding; suffer patiently; also, to continue to exist; to last." Endurance is more than patience, a characteristic we have already discussed.

In the past chapters we have been finding out how love *behaves* — what it does, what its attitudes are. This sentence on love, describing its endurance, its trust, its hope, seems to describe something other than the behavior love produces. It is talking about the *qualities* which are inherent in love. And of course it is apparent at once that those qualities are there only by virtue of having been put there by Christ. Left to ourselves, our love is not always enduring, its trust can be shattered and its hope can be destroyed.

Purely human love is variable. It thrives on appreciation and response and can be withered by neglect or unkindness. Even parental love shares this variability. We have all known parents who loved one child more than the others, or whose love for their children diminished or altered when they were disappointed or hurt by them.

The endurance referred to here is a quality given by God. He is the one from whom we get our endurance. In a sense, He endures us. Nothing about us merits His love. A great deal about us tries the love of our friends and families; how much more must God be repelled by our shabbiness? And yet He loves us. It is not a new concept. Jeremiah the prophet, writing more than six hundred years before Christ, left us this: "The Lord hath appeared of old unto me, saying, Yea, I have loved thee with an everlasting love: therefore with lovingkindness have I drawn thee" (31:3). He was speaking for the Lord to a particularly disobedient and rebellious people, warning them of the terrible events soon to overtake them because of their wickedness. Then — the reminder that, despicable though they were, God still loved them and His chastisement was tempered with mercy.

Seen from our viewpoint the changelessness of God's

love for us is called "grace" or "mercy," or described in the Old Testament as "everlasting love." The timelessness of this love is an integral part of it; it would not be God's love without it. Some people, no doubt, can accept such an out-pouring of undeserved love thankfully and without any inner qualms. But most of us, at some time in our lives, have trouble believing that God could love like that. Why? We all esteem love highly, fervent poetry in praise of its lasting qualities moves us, and yet we can hardly believe it when God offers it to us.

Our difficulties lie deep within our nature. We have minds to think with and imaginations to create with, but we can only create out of things around us and within us. And within us we discover a love that is not changeless but variable. Our ability to love, like everything else about us, is subject to alteration by the behavior of others, by our own fluctuation of mood and even by the state of our health. We are not capable of constancy in love, nor of purpose nor even of good intentions. Finding nothing of unchanging, unfluctuating love within ourselves we cannot easily imagine it to be, even in God. At bottom, that is our human predica-ment: we are creatures involved in a process of change, how then can we comprehend a God who is unchanging?

The gods born out of the fertile imaginations of men, the gods of Norse and Greek mythology, the pagan deities of the ancient world were just like the men whose minds created them. They changed their minds, fought among themselves, were petulant, jealous, vain and ridiculously pleased by flat-tery. And it is interesting to note that Buddhism, although it offers noble ideals, does so not by appealing to a holy God but by conceiving of the Ultimate Fact as a sort of cosmic Nothingness; not super personal, but less than personal. (Those who accuse Christians of "making up" an idea of God out of our own heads might well note these two directions taken by religion apart from the Judeo-Christian tradition.

It hardly seems likely that men would imagine a God who is nothing at all like humans and who insists on approval of and obedience to a moral standard men have always been at great trouble to explain away.)

No, if we could not have imagined for ourselves the God of the Bible, we can hardly be expected to find Him comprehensible. Again and again the Bible makes it plain that the little knowledge we have of God is given us by Him, not discovered by searching on our part. And that is just the way it is with the love which He has for us, and which He "adds" so to speak to our feeble human love. *We do not so much understand His love for us as experience it.* It is this daily awareness of His love for us, unaltered by our behavior (though He deplores it and intends to change it), unaffected by our coldness of heart, which begins to have its effect on our lives.

I think this happens in two ways. First of all, any obedience, any submission of ourselves on our part to God opens the way for Him to do His work in our lives, to transform and revitalize by *coming Himself in His unchanging love* to live in us. There is really no way to talk about what He does in a human life without sounding, on the one hand, impossibly ethereal and "spiritual," or on the other hand a bit mechanical. Of the two, I'd rather try and explain, however haltingly and imperfectly, what God does in plain terms rather than get too high flown. Paul told the Colossians that what had happened to them when they became Christians was that Christ was *in them!* That means His love, His constancy — His endurance really — and all that goes with it, the hope of glory for us, is in us. To try to define it or describe it is obviously impossible, *but we do experience it.*

That is what many pious people mean when they say, "It wasn't me, it was the Holy Spirit." Unfortunately, such a sentence conveys a sort of passivity, almost a kind of absence or abdication on the part of a human being, and that is just what does *not* happen. Christ, living in and working through a person, makes him *more* himself than he was before. So it is with human love. Unable to keep on, to endure, on our own, we find that quality of constancy added (a poor word, but the best the language offers) by Christ. It *is* the Holy Spirit. It is also you, or me, or whoever is willing to let God in.

But there is another way in which the enduring love of God makes a difference in our lives. Something happens to us when we meet with acceptance instead of the rejection we were tensed to face; when we are greeted by a smile rather than with shouted, angry words; when our irritation finds no retaliation. All the combativeness, all the aggression, melts away. You know how it works, as I do, from experience.

When I was a little girl and had done something naughty, something I knew very well I deserved a spanking for, I got myself ready to face the parental wrath. Sometimes I became sulky, sometimes I prepared an elaborate argument in defense of myself, and sometimes I simply braced myself to take my punishment. But whatever I did, I was reacting in advance to what I was sure my mother's response to my misdeeds would be. (Usually I was not disappointed.)

We do this all through life. My husband came home tired and cross, so I snapped back; my children were restless and irritable, so I was cross with them; my friend was in a bad mood, so I cut her short and ended up in a bad mood myself. God simply does not do that. His love is poured out on us eternally, like an endless waterfall, even when we are braced (as we are for human disapproval) for His anger. Meeting His love takes away all the sullenness with which we have faced our own guilt; the defensiveness is gone. No need for defense when one is met by love. There is a liberating, relaxing freedom in accepting God's love and forgiveness which enables us to relax in our attitude toward others. Having found a love in God which endures, we are free to let ours flow, unimpeded by the small blocks which would usually stop it up.

This does not happen overnight, of course. It takes a long, long time for most of us to learn that God's love endures; and an even longer time to let Him have His way in our own lives so that our love endures. We still have our fluctuations, our plateaus — but something is happening. There is a difference. An eternal quality is being added to our lives.

This love, then, of which Paul speaks as being enduring without limit, is a love infused, transformed, constantly given new life by the love of God working in us. We do not so much "get it" (as we think of acquiring a new attribute) as we allow it to happen in us, and when God is working, we are not passive. All of our brains, emotions, and will are involved in active cooperation with God.

Love Trusts

Victorian novels often depicted a character (a secondary character, never the hero) whose wildness and misdeeds involved everyone in the book in the most melodramatic dilemmas. There was usually a mother who, although brokenhearted by her son's waywardness, still trusted that he would turn out all right. Sometimes it was a childhood sweetheart whose angelic purity at last brought the misguided youth to his senses. She had never ceased to trust him, even when all the evidence pointed to his having abandoned all right.

That is the sort of thing that many of us think of when we read the phrase, "no end to its trust." That kind of blind, no-matter-what trust belongs to a simpler, less sophisticated age, we say. We, on the other hand, under no illusions as to the character of man, often view our fellow creatures with a tolerant cynicism. We are never surprised when someone is disclosed to have been less than honorable. Indeed, we are frequently amazed (and somewhat sceptical) at those whose lives are outwardly impeccable.

No doubt the events of the last fifty years — two devastating wars, and the world constantly troubled by little wars in the last two decades — have disposed us to pessimism. On the personal level we are uncomfortably aware that standards once accepted, at least outwardly, by nearly everyone, are now considered outmoded and quaint. Noble aspirations and sentiments are certainly not the common coin of our day. Those of us who are older may tend to view the new world with alarm, while the younger among us, who have always moved in the cynical spirit of the age, are merely blasé. Whatever emotional overtones our cynicism has, most of us are affected by it. How could we not be? It is in the very air around us.

In that state of mind some of the statements in the Bible seem like the naiveté of another age. They were true, possibly, in the days when the world was innocent, but they are surely not for us — we know too much. A trust that never ends? That is least of all possible to accept, we trust no one, not even ourselves.

The only trouble with this superficial reaction to the Bible and what it says about God and man is that it is based on our own kind of innocence born out of a vast ignorance of history.

As a matter of fact, a great many of our dearly held ideas about ourselves and the world are sheer provincialism; a provincialism which knows nothing beyond its own country, its own decade, its own century. We have drawn a one dimensional picture of other times based on required history courses in high school for the most part, and perhaps some casual reading of costume novels. But dig beneath the slick surface of condensed history books and you will find that we are not the first generation to be cynical, disillusioned, without generally accepted moral values, and sceptical of good.

It was to people living in just such a tired society, converts to Christianity out of Roman and Greek culture which was weary and blasé, that the letters to the Corinthian Christians were written. Earlier in the same letter from which we are quoting Paul's great words about love, he had had some severe words to say about the attitude of the church (5:9, 10). The Christians were aware of a flagrant case of sexual immorality among them, involving a young man and his father's wife — and they were not at all horrified. After reading them off for their acceptance of such a situation, Paul instructs them on disciplining the guilty man. Then he makes two fascinating comments, words which convey as clear a picture of the pagan world of that day as an essay on Roman society.

> In my previous letter I said, "Don't mix with the immoral." I didn't mean, of course, that you were to have no contact at all with the immoral of this world, nor with any cheats or thieves or idolaters — for that would mean going out of the world altogether!

Of course it was a wicked world that Corinthian church existed in — a corrupt society which casually accepted moral depravity as being quite normal. Those Christians were not naive, or innocent, or unaware of what life and men are really like. Paul remarks to them a few paragraphs farther on (6:9-11),

> Don't be any under illusion — neither the impurse, the idolater or the adulterer; neither the effeminate, the pervert or the thief; neither the swindler, the drunkard, the foulmouthed, or the rapacious shall have any share in the kingdom of God. *And such men, remember, were some of you!* But you have cleansed yourselves from all that; you have been made whole in spirit; you have been justified in the name of the Lord Jesus and in the very Spirit of our God.

To get a clear picture of the love that knows "no end to its trust," let us remember that Paul wrote about the thoughtless acceptance of immorality, about living in an immoral world, and the stinging reminder that his readers had been sinners of the worst sort — all to the same people in one letter! Paul was not talking about a love that trusts only because it is blind to the nature of man. He was talking to people who knew only too well the depravity men are capable of from first hand and contemporary experience.

How could such people trust anyone — themselves or others — knowing their own past sins, and their proneness to fall into such sins again? How can we trust, when we are aware of the depths of human nature? To understand at all what kind of trust Paul is talking about, we must set his statement in the light both of his own culture and the Roman world to which he wrote. He was very familiar with the words of Jeremiah (17:9, 10) which read,

> The heart is deceitful above all things, and desperately wicked: who can know it? I the Lord search the heart, I try the reins, even to give every man according to his ways, and according to the fruit of his doings.

He surely knew, also, the truth we read in John 2:24, 25: "But Jesus, on his side, did not trust himself to them — for he knew them all. He did not need anyone to tell him what people were like: he understood human nature."

Our idea that people in former ages were less knowledgeable about human nature just will not stand up to the facts. Of all books, the Bible is the most graphic in depicting men in all the nakedness of motive and deed, and in commenting upon man's proclivity toward sin. *But without cynicism.* And therein lies the key to the New Testament view of man, to Paul's words about a love that trusts, and the key to our own understanding of such trust.

It is not that we are so trustworthy, but that *God is trustworthy, and He is working in us!* We know very well how frail, how gossamer thin our virtues are, the imperceptible slide downward of our own natures. The new life Christ has implanted in us often seems sickly, while our sinful tendencies flourish like weeds. That is all true, but it is not all of the truth. The tender plant which is our new nature may be somewhat like a tiny green shoot, poking its head out of a tangle of briers. But it is planted, it is rooted, and God is the gardener. That is our reason for trust, either in our own eventual triumph over evil, or in others. We are sure because we are in Christ, and He will triumph.

This is a realistic trust, the only kind not based on sentimentality or keeping a blind eye toward the facts. It enables us to view our own stumbling progress without despair, and that of others without cynicism. There is nothing new about all of this. We have been taught, over and over again, that our reason for persevering, for not simply giving up, lies in Christ. The peculiar thing is that knowing this, we must constantly guard against a fatal tendency to expect perfection out of human nature. What a hard, unforgiving spirit some people display toward Christians whose weaknesses they do not share! It is as if they said, "You certainly are a miserable failure as a Christian! No one could trust you, after what you've done. *I* have no problem in that area, and since I do not it seems obvious that you just aren't trying. Well, I'll know better than to expect anything of you after this."

The real thought behind such an attitude is never a trust in what God is doing, but a trust in human nature by itself; once that trust is broken nothing can restore it. How many of us say we believe it is Christ in us, our "hope of glory," but who, without ever putting the thought into words, are sure of our own virtue in certain areas of life, and equally distrustful of those whose besetting sins lie in those areas? One woman in my neighborhood used to say complacently, "I'm very frank. I always believe in being honest and open." She was, in fact, frank to the point of unkindness. If there was a weakness in the character of any of her friends, she pointed it out in the most devastating bluntness. She was fond of telling others what she thought they ought to do. Her "frankness" was a camouflage for being mean. When it came to those not equally blunt she always said, "I wouldn't trust her as far as I could see her. Too mealy-mouthed." You see, we tend to put our trust in our own strong points rather than in the Lord. As a result we *distrust* everyone whose strength lies in something else.

The other side of the coin is the scepticism with which we view our own weaknesses. It's possible to be entirely immobilized because we are so sure of our failure. Or to say of someone else, "He won't stick to it, of course; he has never been able to see anything through." In short, it's very difficult for us to believe either that we'll come crashing down some day in one of our "strong" areas, or that we can ever succeed in the weak ones. Our trust is in ourselves, not in Christ at all.

Perhaps it's a good thing that we all fail, once in a while, in the very area we've been most successful in; and that we see unexpected triumphs in places of defeat. Human nature is unpredictable, we say at such times, but the truth is that the way God works is unpredictable and He doesn't intend for us to be too sure of anything but Himself; it's too dangerous for us.

The only position which is free of either cynicism or baseless optimism is an attitude of trust in God. Human nature may fail; you and I or our most reliable friend may fail; but the failure is not a disaster because God, who is trustworthy, never abandons us to our failure, but picks us up, dusts us off and sets us on the path again. Paul, who might have trusted in his own spiritual superiority never boasted of his attainments but said that they were rubbish compared with knowing Christ. So he could deal with the sins and failures of the Christians struggling out of a pagan

culture and reassure them — "He Who calls you is utterly
faithful and He will finish what He has set out to do" (I
Thessalonians 5:24). That is our position today: not a rose-
colored view of man, but a boundless trust in the God who
works in man.

Love Hopes

To talk about the meaning of certain words is extremely
difficult, because the content has been drained out of them,
first by a sentimental and saccharine interpretation and then
by the hammer blow of the history of our century. "Hope"
is one of those words. Naturally the sweetly pretty version of
hope wilted under the ugly realities of two world wars and a
general abandonment of all absolutes. We are all too often
accused of holding, in defiance of all the evidence, to a long
discredited sentimental kind of hope.

Christians may have, at various times, held that pink-
and-white view — but they did not get it from the Bible.
The hope of which Paul writes, that hope which does not
fade, was a vital part of the faith of those early Christians.
We imagine so easily that our world is far worse than it ever
was before; that we, of all people, have seen too much and
know too much to have any hope of the future. But that is
mere provincial conceit, a notional idea refuted by history.
Even if the Roman Empire were not highlighted by such
bizarre pastimes as combat between men and beasts in the
colisseum, gladiators, death as a public spectacle, crucifixions
and palace intrigues and murders, it would still seem, in all
its dirt and sickness and poverty and disregard for life, a
grim world. But then, so would the Middle Ages; or the
Renaissance; or eighteenth-century England; or nineteenth-
century America.

Christians have hope, not because the world is such
a nice place in which to live, but because we believe that

there is a point to living — an end toward which history
draws inexorably. God has a purpose, and we hope in that
purpose. It is alluded to constantly in the Bible, almost on
every page.

> And that is why, in the end, "every tongue shall confess"
> that Jesus Christ is the Lord, to the glory of God the Father.
> The trumpet will sound and the dead shall be raised be-
> yond the reach of corruption, and we who are still alive
> shall suddenly be utterly changed.
> And after that we shall be with him forever.
> Then I saw a new Heaven and a new earth. . . .

There is the reason for the Christian hope — a final redemption, the end of the story in an unimaginable felicity
with Christ. It has nothing to do with the pious wishing
we often mistake for hope. Read the context around the
sentences quoted — from Philippians, I Corinthians, I Thessalonians, and Revelation — especially Paul's. You will see
that Paul went on to encourage Christians to be constant
in doing good, never wearying, never discouraged — not because things might work out well, but because nothing they
did would ever be lost or wasted in the scheme of eternity.
There would be a final solution, and all patient waiting
would be rewarded — in God's time.

Some people disdain such a hope. It causes us to be
dreamers, they say, out of touch with reality, unable to
function properly in this world. Like most jibes, this one is
completely false. Such a hope is the *only* basis for keeping
one's head — and heart — when things go wrong here. Only
by looking beyond the temporal for a reason for our existence
can we really put up with it. The tragic figures are those
who have staked everything on changing society, or human
nature, or both, *now*. They simply cannot face reality
that human nature apart from Christ is unchangeable. Education does not make people better, it only makes them

cleverer; and a clever criminal, whether he be a political tyrant or a thug, is a far worse terror than a stupid one.

Dorothy L. Sayers has observed, in her author's preface to *Man Born to Be King*, that no Christian tragedy is possible; and she is quite right. Tragedy implies no hope — inevitable, unalterable doom. The message of the Bible is that God does have a purpose, that history is moving toward a climax, that fulfillment and climax will be reached when God says the word; and we, living in Christ, are moving with Him toward His eventual triumph. That is what hope is about. If there will be any tragedy when history is finally wound up, and when all things find their proper places in Christ's kingdom, it will be the tragedy of those who have refused to accept the love and welcome of God. But that is not our responsibility. We can safely leave the wrapping-up process to God. Our concern is that we, right now, when nothing seems to be turning out as we had hoped, do not lose our perspective, but live as trustworthy witnesses to His grace. And the only possible perspective is from the vantage point of eventual victory. It keeps us from becoming astigmatic due to the smog and smoke of unhappy events down here.

Love Never Fails

That brings me to the final sentence in this paragraph. "It [the love that endures, trusts, hopes] is the one thing that still stands when all else has fallen." It is with a certain sense of hesitation that I write these words, for I am only too well aware of our human preference for cheery reassurance. But there it is: "when all else has fallen." It does imply that there will come times when everything will crash in on us. A distressing scene to contemplate, but there it is. We live in the kind of a world in which the only constant factor is change, and some of the changes are unhappy ones.

What do we do then? What do we do when the roof falls in?

The roof did fall in on me, literally, last November, and it was like an earthly "second-the-motion" to a spiritual cataclysm. Early in the autumn my husband, looking forward to a prosperous business and anticipating, for the first time in our marriage, freedom from all the expenses of raising and educating children, began to feel tired. After dragging week followed dragging week, came tests and more tests. And then the dreaded word: leukemia. That was the spiritual hammer blow. Having our rain-soaked ceiling fall in on us with a roar in the middle of the night a month later was only a sort of echo.

The important thing about it all was not that we had to face illness and death, overwhelming as that was. Nor that all the looked-for pleasures of the future were abruptly altered. Those things, sad as they are, are not the stuff out of which our lives are made. Our lives are made, literally remade, in Christ — out of His love, His endurance, His gift of trust, our hope in Him. That is the constant factor in a sliding, shifting world. People change. Circumstances change. Old landmarks are gone, the scenery is remade overnight. Life is not an unbroken spiral upwards, but is subject to cataclysmic upheavals. And in all this, the history of a world bent on getting along without God, we Christians are not exempt from the common lot of mankind.

When the roof falls in — that is the time to bring out the precious store of love's trust. No one needs it when everything is going well. Trust is one of those rock-bottom qualities designed for rough wear. The fact that we speak of trust at all implies circumstances which make it difficult. It is, as a matter of fact, faith in battle dress.

Love endures because it is a gift of the God of eternity. It is illumined by trust and hope, for God is in control. Love without these qualities is sentimentality. With endurance, trust and hope it has buoyancy to rise above daily tedium, resilience to survive disaster, and strength to overcome all adversaries.

My husband and I found that the certainty of God's love was stronger than either physical or spiritual cataclysm. Sagging roofs and leukemia are part of *this* world, but love is for eternity.

9. DANGER —
APPROACH
WITH CAUTION

For if there are prophecies they will be fulfilled and done with, if there are "tongues" the need for them will disappear, if there is knowledge it will be swallowed up in truth. For our knowledge is always incomplete and our prophecy is always incomplete, and when the complete comes, that is the end of the incomplete. — I Corinthians 13:8-10

A great part of the difficulties in life — and especially in the Christian world — arises from our predilection for making absolutes out of relative or conditioned laws. This can be seen frequently in children. Johnny has observed that Mother always shouts at him to stop making all that racket but that she never really does more than yell two or three times. Suddenly, counting on that, he is astonished to find her striding into his bedroom in a fine rage and upending him with several painful whacks. What happened? He had made, in his childish little mind, an absolute out of a conditioned law of behavior. What he did not know was that Mother's habit of merely yelling commands from part of her preoccupied mind (the conditioned law) could be transformed by an infuriating clash with the neighbor next door into action on the irritation closest at hand — Johnny.

It may be a while before Johnny makes quite the same mistake again. But because he is human, he will continue to observe the world around him, classify his observations, and draw conclusions. And many of his conclusions will prove to be as mistaken as his absolute law about Mother never spanking.

Mistaken Conclusions

The habit — one might almost call it a compulsion — of classifying and drawing conclusions has resulted in most of the discoveries about the universe in which we live. Human beings have a built-in need for order in life, so we are constantly measuring, weighing and testing, to fit the universe into an orderly pattern. That's good. After all, an orderly universe is only possible if we know there is an orderly God behind and beyond it all.

Our great respect for order, however, can become a snare, even a false concept. We see the results of God's order in the universe and we assume our experience proves these results are absolutes. For instance, men have always doubted the workability of new inventions. Natural law, they said, had always shown that men could not fly or live under water. But others proved them wrong, not by interfering with natural law but by discovering new natural laws which modified the old ones.

We ought to know better by now than to make absolute statements about the universe. Yet we do, and not only about the physical realm. We are just as dogmatic and rigid about the spiritual realm, drawing conclusions and setting up laws based on our partial knowledge.

It often works this way. God has worked in the life of a dissolute person, one formerly given to carousing and loose living; he turns in disgust from his former habits and becomes an ascetic, living on vegetables and nuts and spending all his time in contemplation and prayer. After awhile, if this happens fairly frequently to several people, the notion will have established itself that all spiritual men will eat vegetables and nuts and spend all their time in contemplation and prayer.

The principle can be narrowed down. In a certain church the leaders seem to use certain phrases in their prayers and give testimonies replete with certain spiritual "sayings." The congregation gets the idea that this is what a really spiritual person talks like, this is how he prays. And the first thing you know everybody is talking the same jargon, a jargon born, perhaps, out of genuine experience in one man's life but filtered through successive imitators until it has become a cliché — slick talk, ecclesiastical style.

It seems to me it is this kind of classifying that Paul was warning against when he wrote the paragraph quoted at the beginning of this chapter. In essence, he was saying that there are absolutes, the love of God is an absolute, but God works in various ways and through many methods; and let us not mistake the method for the principle behind it. The methods God uses are suited to our temporal condition — an ever-changing, ever-shifting condition. They will, one day, be abandoned forever.

There have always been three strands woven into the life of God's people; the prophetic, the ecstatic, and the didactic (the last is simply an impressive word for teaching). The three seem to have progressed at an uneven pace. Sometimes one strand has predominated, sometimes another, but all three have always been there. Paul reminds us that the need for them will eventually end. There are two ways in which we can twist the truth behind these "methods" of the Holy Spirit into falsehood. One is by measuring the spiritual health of the church by the prevalence of any one of them; and the other is by declaring that the time for one or all of them is gone. Neither is a true conclusion.

All of them, prophecy and ecstatic utterance and the pursuit of knowledge, imply an incompleteness to life. We do not know the future, either in the sense of foreseeing God's hand in history or of seeing the end result of our own decisions. A great part of the world's misery is the result of the miscalculations of men as to the results of certain deeds. This inability to predict what will happen if the present step is taken extends from the rulers of nations to each one of us.

Prophecy is, in a sense, God's occasional reply to our finiteness. Sometimes it has been proclaiming the Word of God; sometimes it has been inspired foretelling of the future; always it is designed to bring God's people to a right relationship to Him, to recall them to godly conduct or to give them courage in difficulty. It is easy to see why Paul said prophecy would be fulfilled and done with. It belongs to this age of incompleteness which will one day be swallowed up in God's finality.

"Tongues," or ecstatic experiences of any kind, have always been rather difficult for those who have not experienced them to comprehend. And there has often been an unwillingness to admit their validity. On the other hand, those who have had these experiences find them so meaningful that they feel everyone should have them. Each side has numerous Scripture references to bolster its position. Armed with arguments, Biblical texts, and appeals to the evidence, both sides are soon busy analyzing and measuring and weighing and dividing as if Christianity were a set of propositions instead of a response to God's revelation of Himself.

The tiniest bit of the love Paul has been describing

would go a long way toward making such disputes cease,
and that is what he recommends. How different the history
of the Church — and of individual lives — would have been
if the preeminence had been placed on love rather than on
other attributes.

As for knowledge, its opposite is ignorance; both will be
"swallowed up" in truth.

Paul's treatment of prophecy, tongues and knowledge
stresses that all are necessary to us in our state of incompleteness — and all are potentially dangerous. Any one of
them can lead to an overbearing pride, a sort of spiritual
smugness which is a deadlier temptation to Christians than
the grossest carnal sins. If you doubt this, think for a moment
of the most aggravating Christian you know. The likelihood
is that he — or she — is infuriating not because of a lack of
virtue but because of pretensions to perfection. Furthermore,
we find ourselves annoyed by them because we see ourselves — our own secret and despised vainness and conceit
— in them.

I once knew a young man who was extremely trying to
his family and friends because he always forgave them whenever he had done anything wrong. Nothing is more infuriating than the bland assumption that one's own foibles
and failures are really the work, or the fault, of others —
especially if it is accompanied by a tolerant forgiveness. I
think the reason I found him so exasperating was that I saw
in him my own inner self excusing and explaining away
my bad temper, my evasions of the truth, my selfishness,
my blaming others. The thing I could not bear to admit
as my own sin was the very thing I disliked most in others.

You know the sort of thing we do: "Of course it was
inexcusable to jump on Donna that way, but really the child
had been so trying all day that I was beside myself"; or,
"I know it was a white lie, but really one can't speak honestly to her — she flies into a temper at the least hint of

criticism, and you *know* I can't stand a scene." Well, there it is. Little, petty, niggardly sins. We are all guilt of them and we all loathe ourselves for it.

The safest, indeed, the only thing to do when we find ourselves fallen once again into the old, habitual sin, is to run, not walk, to God in confession and be renewed by His forgiveness. It is also the hardest thing to do. What, in fact, we usually do is to turn from the uncomfortable confrontation with God; we do not want even a forgiving, loving, merciful God at such times. We want to have our embarrassment soothed, our pride restored. So we justify ourselves and then turn to something which will help us to forget the awkward and uncomfortable feeling of failure.

And that is the great point of danger — that we will embrace teaching, an ecstatic experience, or a devotion to knowledge — anything, so long as we can keep from dealing with our inability to be what we ought to be.

Misplaced Standards

I know that there are Bible students who will, at this point, accuse me of playing ducks and drakes with the Word of God. They feel, and rightly so, that the Bible, as God's divinely revealed Word, demands serious and reverent consideration, for it contains all we need to know of His revealed truth. They often approach it somewhat in the manner of a cryptographer studying a code — every word, every phrase must be analyzed, compared, searched for deep meanings.

I couldn't agree more with the need for taking the Bible seriously as the Word of God. But there is a pitfall in the viewpoint which in laying equal stress on each sentence of the Bible searches for the ultimate meaning of each phrase, as if through a spiritual microscope; one may easily miss the *message* of the Bible. It was, after all, spoken — and written — to plain, ordinary, usually uncomplicated men and women, and was meant for them to understand. Even the hyperbole and the poetic fervor of the prophets with its element of mystery was primarily intended to convey a message. When the Lord, speaking through Ezekiel, thundered out His wrath against Judea for her sins, it was not to construct an elaborate theological proposition for the priests to work out, but to tell God's people that if they didn't "shape up" they were in for trouble:

> Therefore thus says the Lord God: Because you are more turbulent than the nations that are round about you, and have not walked in my statutes or kept my ordinances, but have acted according to the ordinances of the nations that are around about you; therefore thus says the Lord God: Behold, I, even I, am against you; and I will execute judgments in the midst of you in the sight of the nations. And because of all your abominations I will do with you what I have never yet done, and the like of which I will never do again (5:7, 8).

It is true there are enough obscure passages, hard to comprehend. But then there is certainly enough plain teaching to keep us all busy bringing our lives into conformity with it. It is *full* of quite obvious teaching. Do this; do not do that; behave this way not that way.

Why is it, then, that a great many people would rather pore over the obscure passages in the Bible rather than the greater part of it which is unmistakeable in its meaning? And why is it that all Christian groups tend to make one bit of teaching the criterion by which a man is judged to be, or not to be, a Christian — often to the exclusion of other teaching?

There are, for instance, some people who consider divorce, especially if it is followed by remarriage, to be a sin so terrible that it can never be forgiven in this world or the next. Those who commit it are always regarded as second class Christians. There is no doubt but that Jesus regarded divorce as the breaking of a relationship upon which God has set His seal, and as such, an evidence of human sinfulness. But His teaching on the use and inordinate love of money, and on greed and selfishness, takes up far, far more space in the gospels than anything He said about divorce. Furthermore, much of what He had to say about a man's attitudes toward his possessions equated that attitude with his basic motivation in life. Consider these remarks:

"Don't pile up treasures on earth, where moth and rust can spoil them and thieves can break in and steal. . . . For wherever your treasure is, you may be certain that your heart will be there too! . . . No one can be loyal to two masters. He is bound to hate one and love the other, or support one and despise the other. You cannot serve God and the power of money at the same time."

"Believe me, a rich man will find it very difficult to enter the kingdom of Heaven. Yes, I repeat, a camel could more easily squeeze through the eye of a needle than a rich man get into the kingdom of God!"

"Have you no eyes — which is more important, the gift, or the altar which sanctifies the gift?" ". . . be on your guard against covetousness in any shape or form. For a man's real life in no way depends upon the number of his possessions."

"The man who is faithful in the little things will be faithful in the big things, and the man who cheats in the little things will cheat in the big things too. So that if you are not fit to be trusted to deal with the wicked wealth of this world, who will trust you with the true riches? And if you are not trustworthy with someone else's property, who will give you property of your own?"[1]

Then there are so many references to honesty, trustworthiness, and responsibility in dealing with possessions

---

[1]Matthew 6:19, 21, 24; 19:23, 24; 23:19; Luke 12:15; 16:10-12.

that one could hardly enumerate them all. It should be enough to remember that Paul spent almost an entire chapter in his first letter to Timothy warning him that putting money first can be a deadly danger to the soul.

How odd it seems, in view of the New Testament's stress upon our attitude toward material things and upon one loving "the brethren" as the evidence of our faith, that the church should continually be veering off in the direction of other emphases — not least of which is the setting up of spiritual "gifts" or special knowledge, as criteria of judgment. It reminds me of my childhood. I remember very well that whenever I had done something wrong and thought my mother might punish me for it I hastened to bring to her attention my brother's misdeeds. That is just what we all too often do in the Christian world. Rather than face, and deal with, the sins that are our own, we look around for some evidence of someone else's sin. And to complete the whitewash we point with pride to our faithfulness as a Sunday school or Bible teacher, or our spirituality as shown by some "gift."

The happily married man deplores divorce; the rich man whose questionable business practices have made the Church a scandal to the secular world rises to heights of eloquence in condemning worldly amusements; the self-righteous woman whose tongue is a terror to her associates can be depended upon to broadcast the sins and failures of others. And so it goes. We are always turning the message of the Bible into a classified list of rules, with the stress upon those which don't (we think) affect our lives.

The Judgment of Love

At the moment in which I find myself deciding that so-and-so has committed a sin I must do two things. First, I must ask myself if this is a sin I have found in myself and hate to face. If it is, I must pray for forgiveness for myself, and for my fellow Christian caught in the same trap. If it is not a sin I have committed, I must ask myself whether my own sins are not just as deadly and if I am using someone else's failure to mask my own. And again, I must pray for forgiveness for myself, and for the ability to see my own sins as clearly as I see others'; and for the other person, who needs my prayers not my judgment.

One of the ways in which the love of God works itself out in our lives is by giving us concern, not condemnation, for each other.

We are never detached in our attitude toward those we love. They may make us furious, at times, but we care about them, and what they do and what they become. Their sins may wound us, but only because we do love them. That concern born out of love can be healing. It causes us to pray, to do all we can to help each other, and to turn the searchlight of judgment on ourselves, not others.

There will always be the sweet, subtle temptation to pride through knowledge, or ability, or spirituality. But we might well remember that on the last night Jesus spent with His disciples, He talked a great deal about love — His for us, the Father's love for us in Him, ours for Him and for each other. He touched on it again and again, as if to impress it upon the disciples' minds. He did not give them a handy set of rules to follow; He simply pointed out that loving Him meant following His commandments. The evidence of that love would be seen by the world in the love Christians have for each other.

Some of the things we are so impressed by — intellectual attainments, specialized knowledge, the ability to speak and to teach — will be done away with some day . . . no need for them in heaven. But love, unlike knowledge, will simply increase. What we have now is the bud. Then we will have the flower.

10. GROW
UP!

When I was a little child I talked and felt and thought like a little child. Now that I am a man my childish speech and feeling and thought have no further significance for me.

— I Corinthians 13:11

I always used to be puzzled by Paul's insistence in I Corinthians 13:11 on leaving childhood behind. How could this be reconciled with what Jesus said about receiving the kingdom of God as a little child and becoming like little children in order to enter the kingdom (Luke 18:17; Matthew 18:3)? On the one hand Jesus seems to be recommending a simple, childlike view of life. On the other hand, Paul advocates subtle, complex thinking only an adult can grasp.

The difficulty, however, was not between Paul and Jesus but with me. I was doing what I cautioned against in the last chapter — trying to construct a system out of one observation. In each case I was making a theology out of an illustration, and we all know that illustrations can't be pushed too far or they collapse. In commending the simplicity with which children accept life — father, mother, the shape and smell and sound of the familiar neighborhood — Jesus was telling us to accept God's entry into our lives with the same simplicity. This was His reply to the disciples' question about who was greatest in the kingdom of Heaven. Children do not think in terms of greatness or social status or "being better than," until they grow into it, until their simplicity is eroded by the adult world of values.

Jesus then added that anyone who led little children astray would be better off dead. From that terrible statement He plunged into a sober warning about the high cost of faith which sometimes even requires the lopping off of hand or foot (Matthew 18:1-9). From His use of little children as examples of uncomplicated acceptance of God and His universe, we must not construct any theologies unbalanced by the rest of His teaching. He also told His followers to be as wise as serpents and gentle as doves; to take up their cross and follow Him; to treat men exactly as they would like to be treated; to love their enemies. Children, for all their simplicity, do not do that. Half an hour spent watching a group of tots playing together — the single-minded contention for possession of toys, the tears of rage when one has what the other wants, the simple, uncomplicated blows and kicks — should convince us that it is not *that* kind of childishness Jesus is recommending. Nor did He advise us to think on a childish level, which would be to divest ourselves of all we learn by experience and study — a slander, incidentally, that outsiders often level against us.

Jesus' loving care of children and His praise of their openness do not conflict with the words of Paul: "Now that I am a man my childish speech and feeling and thought have no further significance for me." They refer to two different things. In order to get at the heart of the matter, we must first decide what exactly they do refer to.

In the first instance, Jesus was talking about the kingdom of Heaven, the qualifications for getting there and (in the disciples' minds) being "greatest" there. The disciples were thinking, as the Pharisees did, in terms of *earning* a place of honor before God. We often use the Pharisees' attempts to earn their salvation as an example of the worst kind of human arrogance, as if they deliberately twisted the truths of the Old Testament to arrive at their position. Their mistaken idea of earning God's approval, however, seems to have been a universal one. Nor are we exempt. We do it too — more subtly. When Jesus told the disciples that, contrary to their ideas of earned glory, the only way to enter the kingdom was to accept it, simply, as a little child accepts gifts, He was speaking to us.

Children love presents, and accept them without asking why. I don't believe they even think about why they should be given presents until we put ideas into their heads: "Be a good boy, and I'll bring you something from town." Without that indoctrination they never ask why we give them gifts. They just receive openly. We, on the other hand, have learned to think in terms of our "rights," of what is due us. All too soon we come to take even gifts as being no more than our due — because we are so good, or have worked so hard, or are so charming or so beautiful, or so . . . on and on. Women expect admiration from men; haven't they worked for hours on hair and skin and clothes to "earn" admiration? So it is, so it has become in the adult world. We delude ourselves that everything we have has come because of our intrinsic worth — even our standing before God.

In a few sentences, Jesus struck that idea out. God is gracious. He has come to us, not we to Him. Nothing we get from His hand is the reward for our goodness; there isn't any, either goodness or reward. The earth we walk on, the air we breathe, everything about us is God's creation. Our part has been to misuse it all until we have become hopelessly lost. God has come to us and given us His salvation in Christ, just the way a loving parent gives food and clothing and care to his child.

In the illustration of a child's faith, Jesus was using the strongest picture He could find, the thing most opposite to the Pharisees' (and the disciples') ideas of earned reward. Everyone knows that children are dependent on the care of grownups; they don't earn the care. We are like children before God. *Everything we have is God's gift to us and is unearned.* That is the point of Jesus' illustration.

A Child Is Undisciplined

Paul, however, is concerned that we become adult in our view of ourselves and our world. On the one hand he has been talking about the limited nature of our lives and our knowledge, contrasting it with the fulfillment of seeing God. When we claim that we know "God's secrets," that our knowledge is complete, we are acting childishly. Children are not aware of the vast areas of knowledge outside their experience; that awareness is part of growing up. Children react simply and unthinkingly on the basis of all they know, and for them that "all" is all there is. That is why learning is always a painful process — it hurts to find how little we know. The prophecies, tongues, knowledge of which Paul spoke belong to this incomplete age, where we do *not* know everything.

On the other hand, Paul has been talking about love — how it acts, what its attitudes are, how it supersedes knowledge. There are childish reactions — feelings, talk, thoughts — that are not compatible with the love Paul describes and which must be put away. Children are not only simple, uncomplicated, dependent without question. They are also creatures of instinct. They do not yet act responsibly. When they are petted and loved they respond with affection; when they are thwarted or hurt they respond with tears and rage. Who has not seen some captivating toddler, restrained by his mother from throwing his food on the floor, respond by hitting at her with his little fists? Even babies, when they don't get what they want, will cry and kick and strike out. "Bad mommy!" one little boy used to say every time his mother disciplined him.

Babies take no responsibility for themselves. All is laid upon others, and for babies that is all right. But the whole point of training, of educating our children, is to teach them to take responsibility for themselves, and ultimately for others. We teach them that they must not react instinctively to the irritations and frustrations of life. Adults who are truly mature do not strike out blindly when they don't like what happens to them. Those who do are simply reacting on the old childish level.

Love is a universal human experience. Children love, freely and in response to love. When one becomes an adult, that love must be transformed from instinctual into responsible love. All the qualifications of love Paul has been talking about are descriptions of what love is like when it is responsible. Growing up doesn't mean we no longer have the emotions and instincts we had as children. It does mean that they must be developed and trained and disciplined so as to be fully realized.

I suppose everyone knows at least one person who has balked at growing up. Some years ago my husband and I met an attractive couple to whom we were much drawn. After a few dinners together, however, we found our enthusiasm for our new acquaintances shrinking away. Underneath the charm, the husband was a big baby. He seldom stayed more than a few months in any job because the boss turned out to be a tyrant who expected him to really work eight hours a day. Or else no one recognized his abilities and treated him with respect. Or the work was just *too* grueling for someone of his caliber. He pouted when his wife failed to fix his favorite food and looked at her with the uncomprehending hurt face of a child when she was cross because he played golf on moving day. He was as sunny, as artlessly amusing, and as irresponsible as a child. And his Christian faith was just as undeveloped.

When, driven beyond endurance, his wife remonstrated with him, reminding him of their commitment to maintain a home and raise their children, she was answered with, "You seem to forget, Claudia, that the man is the head of the house. If you'd only realize that and stop nagging me about money. A really spiritual woman would be satisfied with the simple, wholesome things of life. You spend too much time thinking about things . . ." (He bought his clothes at the most exclusive men's shop in town.)

No, he wasn't a stupid man, nor was he deliberately, knowingly selfish. He simply thought like a child. He was the center of the universe, and he *honestly* could not understand that other people's lives were as important as his. To try to get him to see someone else's point of view gave one the sensation of talking to a wax figure. There was no response, nothing was heard. He usually answered such arguments by saying, "But I needed it . . . but I didn't want to . . . but I was tired." I may not have mentioned how nice he was when everything went his way — but it was so tiring keeping everything going his way.

True, he was an extreme example, but we all know men and women who are very like this man — still children emotionally and spiritually, as if at some point in their lives all growth stopped. Their inability to see that other people's rights are as important as their own is genuine — inexcusable but real. It can go hand in hand with an almost nauseating spirituality, side by side but never converging. Such people often love to give testimonies or pray publicly, though they are never found working behind the scenes. On second thought, their spirituality *is* nauseating; it has the sickly sweetness of cotton candy, and is just as insubstantial.

One thing these people all have in common: they have never submitted to any discipline, either from others or from themselves. Only the constant process of applied discipline makes children into adults. Left to himself, no child would ever learn anything. Learning is hard work, mentally and physically, and the rewards are often not obvious. How much pleasanter to stay sticky and dirty, to run unrestrained by time limits and baths and lessons! Learning is always painful. Only later, from the vantage point of maturity, does the process appear worthwhile.

A Child Is Self-Centered

Those of you who have gone through this maturing, learning process, or who are now painfully taking small children through it, are no doubt thinking, "Yes, all very true. I can see the necessity of disciplining and training a child. But that's just common sense. What's it got to do with Christianity?"

It has everything to do with it. The evidence of both the Bible and our own lives tells us that as Christians we grow in much the same way that we do on the human level. First babyhood, the simple uncluttered idea that *my* salvation, *my* prayers, *my* happiness are the supreme concerns of God and His angels. Then, haltingly and with many pauses, comes the process of growth. We begin to turn our attention outward, to see others — *really* see them — as loving, hating, needing, fearing beings like ourselves. We begin dimly to apprehend something of the grace of God in coming to us, loving us. Our self-absorption is broken by genuine concern for others.

And so the slow, tedious, often painful business of growing up into Christian maturity goes on — unless we stop it. It's possible, at any place along the way, to dig our heels in and go no further. The by-paths of the Christian life are littered with Christians who have done just that. How many times have I, in just such petulant childishness, indulged in a fit of spiritual sulking because my desires were thwarted! It's fatally easy to look around at other Christians who seem to be far better off, to be sailing through life on smooth seas with no difficulties, no sudden stops, no crushing disappointments — and to sink into self-pity.

Children are always measuring what they have by others. They are quick to howl if they think someone else is getting ahead of them. "You gave him a bigger piece than me!" "You always let Mary do what she wants and I never get to do *anything* I want!" I would guess that about half the time parents spend arbitrating their children's quarrels has to do with this kind of comparison.

This single-minded view of oneself as the center of the universe, which naturally leads one to avoid all responsibility (for accepting responsibility comes with awareness of the rights of others) and produces jealousy for one's own rights and privileges, is normal for children. But when it is never outgrown, when it remains the chief characteristic of an adult, then it is abnormal, a kind of spiritual and emotional retardation. The simple truth is that we must grow up. We cannot stay children forever, for the very things that are endearing in a child are a horror in an adult. Just as the very shape of a person changes as he grows from baby fat and cuddliness to adult proportions, just as his behavior changes from gurgles and formless noises to words and sentences, so his inner shape ought to change and grow. The emotional postures of childhood are grotesque when childhood is gone.

A great deal of our ineffectiveness as Christian witnesses in the world is due to our spiritual babyishness, single-minded in its focus on self. We are fascinated with discussions on the devotional life and prayer, not because we need both to maintain and deepen our relationship with the Lord, but because we want to be spiritually superior. We witness, not out of a genuine concern for others, but because we want to appear, to ourselves and others, bathed in the glow of sanctification. We are children, showing off before each other — and before God.

There is the danger that testimony meetings become nothing more than boasting contests — sort of a pious "can you top this" contest. Are we motivated, when we give a testimony, by a desire to make plain the goodness and mercy of God? Or is the secret desire really to gain status in the particular group we're anxious to impress? It may be possible to want only to glorify the Lord, but, prone as we are to self love and conceit, it is possible that at times our motives are mixed. The danger is that more and more we will be impelled to speak by a secret wish to enhance our spiritual status in the group.

This is not to say all testimonies are bad. Much help can be gotten from hearing what God has done in someone's life. But great care must be exercised to avoid the danger of falling into the sin of self-congratulation and pride. Of course, there is danger in anything we do in life. We are always a knife-edge away from falling either into sloth and complacency (one side of the ditch) or pride and censoriousness (the other side of the ditch).

It is even dangerous to pray. The devil lurks at our shoulder to tell us, as we rise from our knees, "How spiritual you are! What lovely feelings you had as you prayed! Indeed, you are a rare soul!" Of course, we can't avoid all danger, we must accept the risk there is in living and go on doing the best we can, knowing that God will set us straight if we get out of line. And that is much of what maturity is.

A Child Is Unrealistic

A child can be selfish — in a simple, uncomplicated way — and quite frankly conceited. He demands that life conform to his little needs, because he doesn't know much of reality. His little world, bounded by the horizons of home and neighborhood, is not at all like the real world outside. He is protected from the dangers of that real world by his family. Growing up means learning that the real world is there, and what it really is.

We cannot, as Christians, continue to be bounded by our childish world, only venturing out occasionally to "witness" to the inhabitants of that *other* world, then dashing back to the safety of the ghetto. Being spiritually adult means getting out into the world as it is and living there as Christians. The kind of witnessing we are expected to do is the hard, unglamorous, untalked of witnessing of simply *being* Christ's men and women. A witness is one who gives evidence. Our lives ought to give evidence of our faith. We always like to stress giving evidence in terms of speaking for Christ. That is part of it. But not the trumped up, artificial kind of speaking which is imposed upon a conversation so that we can go back to our church and tell what we did. That's like a little boy coming home to tell Mama what a good boy he was in school that day.

This is not a polemic against testimony meetings or witnessing — only a protest against their misuse. We Christians are a minority whose allegiance to Christ makes our attitudes and goals sharply different, in some cases opposite, to those of the world we live in. We do need each other. But Christ sent us out into the world to be His people. That means we must have a genuine point of contact with our world. We can't be so different in appearance and behavior that there is no meeting ground. The difference is inward, in the set of our lives. We are committed to Christ in a way that involves our whole being and radically alters our goals and attitudes.

Because there is a tension in living a daily life in a world diametrically opposed — or at best indifferent — to what is most important to us, we need to have times to be with other Christians. We need to meet together regularly for mutual encouragement, for fellowship, for worship, as our Lord commanded us. Together we bear one another's burdens, rejoice with one another, and gain strength for tomorrow. That is what all our meetings are for. Life is balanced: our normal daily life carried on in the world, being Christ's men and women; our times of drawing together as a specifically Christian group, to refuel, as it were; then out into the world again.

The danger is that we may reverse the order. We may do all of our real living strictly within the confines of the Christian ghetto, merely making little forays out into the world, then dashing back with stories of our prowess as "witnesses" for Christ, when all the time there has been no real contact made. We may become so absorbed in our pleasant life within the framework of our fellowship that we are aware of the rest of the world only at the fringes of our minds.

You think this is exaggerated? I know dozens, hundreds, of Christians — earnest, sincere people who, as they would say, "love the Lord," yet they never even *see* the world in which they live. *That* is the kind of childish thinking Paul says the adult must put away. A child sees the world in relationship to himself. So do too many Christians. We label people and then stop thinking about them. In our minds they have large signs printed on their foreheads: "Worldly Man — drinks too much"; "Nominal Christian — probably not born again (he doesn't use the same clichés I use)"; "Sophisticated Pagan — he discusses Sartre and Tillich, obviously a dangerous thinker." And so on.

In order for Christ's purpose to be accomplished and men and women brought into His kingdom, His people must go out and get them. It is as simple as that. There is only one way to get them. We must meet people as individuals, give ourselves to them in genuine interest and friendship — not in order to "save" them, but because we like them. We are to be the salt of the earth in our daily lives, preserving and flavoring the society in which we live. When the time is ripe, when our friends are ready to look into this business of Christianity, they'll turn to us. *We* do not manipulate, nor choose. God manipulates and chooses times and methods. All we are to do is to be so thoroughly His in motive and action that we're usable, ready at the right time. We might take our cue from Paul's advice to the Christians at Colossae:

> Be wise in your behavior towards non-Christians, and make the best possible use of your time. Speak pleasantly to them, *but never sentimentally*, and learn how to give a proper answer to every questioner (Colossians 4:5, 6, italics mine).

The picture the New Testament gives of Christian witnessing, as these words indicate, is that of mature people whose lives embody a quality which in itself is evidence of goodness. When men are aware of their own need, they'll ask. We are to be ready with an answer. We are to be *there* — where they are, facing the temptations they face, living under the pressures they live under, but in a manner that proclaims another allegiance than they have. That is witnessing. Without the validity of our lives, our words are nothing.

What good does it do for us to be constantly trotting out our little homilies about what Christ has done for us, or the joys of being born again, if we are just as obsessed by status as the most careless pagan, just as sloppy in our business ethics, just as vicious in our gossip? After all, people in our culture are used to advertising. Witnessing without commitment to the hard ethics of the New Testament, without involvement and concern for people, is just another "hard sell," on a par with touting a superior brand of soap, or a new toothpaste.

Children are so simple in their bragging. "My Dad is smarter than your Dad." "Our car is bigger than your car." Let's not put the Gospel on that level. An adult is one who has insight enough to look at himself and others honestly, and to meet them openly. We've got to grow up, first of all, into responsibility. The universe does not center around us but around Christ, and others are important to Him. Every human being whom we meet has hopes, fears, sorrows, longings, just as we do. Everyone is looking for recognition and acceptance. Children see people as figures either clear and distinct or receding into the background according to whether or not the figures "do something" for them. We, as responsible Christian adults, must see people as three dimensional, recognize them and accept them, before we can witness to them.

And that is one of the very real qualities of love. You can't love what you don't know. We won't have any love to give to others until we see them clearly, know them as friends and accept them as part of our lives. I remember how, as a little girl, I played with my friends. We used to begin by saying, "Let's play like . . ." and then we went at it. We played house, we played cowboys and Indians, we played all sorts of games — but they were only games. When dinner time came we dropped our pretense and went home. Sometimes that is the way we appear to the world. We play at being charming, being sweet and understanding, but the game is very short. The moment passes, we turn and go home — to our real lives, our own friends, our families, our familiar church groups — and nothing has been changed. The "outsiders" are still on the outside, and they know it.

Growing Up to the Pattern

We have a pattern for living and witnessing. Jesus witnessed to us of the Father's love:

> For we have no superhuman High Priest to whom our weaknesses are unintelligible — he himself has shared fully in all our experience of temptation, except that he never sinned.
>
> Let us therefore approach the throne of grace with fullest confidence, that we may receive mercy for our failures and grace to help in the hour of need (Hebrews 4:15, 16).

That is the way Christ did it — He came to us.

Paul carried the pattern out in this way (I Corinthians 9:19-22):

> For though I am no man's slave, yet I have made myself everyone's slave, that I might win more men to Christ. To the Jews I was a Jew, that I might win the Jews. To those who were under the Law I put myself in the position of being under the Law (although in fact I stand free of it), that I might win them who are under the Law. To those who had no Law I myself became like a man without the Law (even though in fact I cannot be a lawless man for I am bound by the law of Christ), so that I might win the men who have no Law. To the weak I became a weak man, that I might win the weak. I have, in short, been all things to all sorts of men that by every possible means I might win some to God.

We must give up our childish playing with witnessing, come out of the safety of our little Christian sub-society and meet men where they are — really *meet* them. When we do that, when we live for Christ right out in the open, we'll be witnessing all right. We'll be speaking to men and women about Jesus Christ, not artificially and by contrived means, but because they'll be ready to hear. But you can be sure of this — we will be doing a lot more *living* than talking.

11. GOD'S
SECRETS

At present we are men looking at puzzling reflections in a mirror. The time will come when we shall see reality whole and face to face! At present all I know is a little fraction of the truth, but the time will come when I shall know it as fully as God now knows me!   — I Corinthians 13:12

Have you ever felt a delicious shiver as you get well into a good mystery story? Will you ever forget the delight with which you plunged into fairy tales, let's pretend games, or imagined you were seeing another, more mysterious and beautiful world as twilight worked its magic? Have your sensibilities ever been ruffled by the brassy, over-confident voice of the man who is always telling how the trick is done?

Those who have never experienced these things will not understand this chapter at all. But I think there will not be many of them, for most of us will acknowledge that this realm of the fantasy world is a great part of our lives.

Some of us have tried to outgrow it and succeeded well enough to become very pedestrian. Some of us are ashamed of it and hide our penchant for mystery stories or fairy tales as if it were a sin. Some of us have filed it away in a dark corner of our memories, sorry the world is, after all, such a gray, plodding place. But perhaps the best thing to do is to admit that our inborn love of mystery, our deep sense of an unseen world around us, is part of our nature, and therefore given by God. It may be (since we are all sinners) tinged with the flaw that all our nature bears, but it is a good thing spoiled, and it points to something good.

Paul was well aware of this, and allusions to his awareness flash out now and again in his writing. Perhaps the first-century world was not so smothered with an overlay of sophistication as ours is, was more in harmony with the created world. Paul certainly wrote as if he expected his readers to understand his references.

The Mysterious Universe

The quotation at the beginning of the chapter spells it out in so many words. We do not understand our world, nor ourselves; we are mysteries, living in a mystery, knowing a tiny part of the truth, but looking forward one day to seeing it all clearly. Writing to the Christians at Rome and encouraging them to give themselves wholly to Christ in a time of difficulty and suffering, Paul links the future of the whole created world with our triumph in Christ (8: 19-23):

> The whole creation is on tiptoe to see the wonderful sight of the sons of God coming into their own. The world of creation cannot as yet see reality, not because it chooses to be blind, but because in God's purpose it has been so limited — yet it has been given hope. And the hope is that in the end the whole of created life will be rescued from the

tyranny of change and decay, and have its share in that magnificent liberty which can only belong to the children of God!

It is plain to anyone with eyes to see that at the present time all created life groans in a sort of universal travail. And it is plain, too, that we who have a foretaste of the Spirit are in a state of painful tension, while we wait for that redemption of our bodies which will mean that at least we have realized our full sonship in him.

In the same vein Paul wrote, "For we are looking all the time not at the visible things, but at the invisible. The visible things are transitory: it is the invisible things that are really permanent" (II Corinthians 4:18). Considering that the Bible is a book about a mystery (God's love and redemption for us), and that the air of another world than ours breathes through every page of it with hints now and again of glories too great for us to know yet, one would think that Christians would, of all people, be respectful of things God has kept hidden. But no, all too often we crush secret longings and stamp down all wonder and delight in God's universe, by dividing everything up into tidy bundles about which we know "everything," reducing all to sterile and deadly neatness. We behave as though our chief end in life were to reduce all the world and the people in it to a set of specifications — everyone labeled, categorized, memorized and filed away to be forgotten. We act as though having enough information would bring everyone to a knowledge of Christ. We even attempt to capture all the indefinable vagaries of man's awakening to God's call in a formula: a series of questions and answers, as cut and dried as a mathematical equation. Perhaps that is why, however earnest such efforts to bring people to Christ may be, they are often unproductive.

We are frequently guilty of treating God's world and

His people as if they were units in a gigantic mechanism to which we have the key. All that is needed is a look at the master sheet to pop everything into the proper slot. We act as if all the secrets of the universe, as well as the mysteries of God's dealings with people, were an open book to us. The conceit is nothing new. The Pharisees thought along the same lines, and had their rules to cover everything. It was to one of them that Jesus said, "The wind blows where it likes, you can hear the sound of it but you have no idea where it comes from and where it goes. Nor can you tell how a man is born by the wind of the Spirit" (John 3:8).

A Systematized World

There seem to be two opposing longings in man. One is the sense of wonder and awe at this vast, incomprehensible universe in which we live. The other is the urge to reduce it all to a system. The first, if not controlled and directed, can degenerate into a fascination with mystery or magic and eventually lead one into the dark realms of the occult. The second causes us to regard others as things rather than people and to treat them impersonally. In doing both we miss the message God has put into the universe. Since our age is one of scepticism regarding the supernatural coupled with a reverent attitude toward the scientific method, today we inevitably drift into a preoccupation with systems and classification.

I once met a young man who took a very dim view of Christianity. He was rather hopelessly searching for some sort of answer to life's mysteries, but felt there was nothing for him in the Christian faith. When I had talked with him for a while, I found that on three occasions he had been "led to the Lord" by eager exponents of the sort who reduce the whole of the Gospel to a questions-and-answer system. He responded, apparently, to the answers with the

"next question" on the list, and so the little procedure went
along until he was converted — according to those who were
"counseling" him.

The trouble was that, though the system was successful
according to those who were "using it" on him (and how
like a *thing* that makes him sound) it really didn't work.
Nothing happened. It seems to me that those who use that
sort of method — and I find even the word "method" in
connection with such a personal matter as one's faith very
distasteful — must have all their attention focused on their
little system so that they are terribly insensitive to the person himself.

When we treat human beings as objects to be "witnessed to" or "converted," rather than people, we are giving them a stone instead of bread — something completely
out of character for God. Having created us all infinitely
different from each other, He respects our individuality and
deals with each one of us differently. Jesus never reduced
His relationships with people to a system — ask me A and
I'll answer A-1, then we'll go on to question B. He did
them the honor of *seeing* them and meeting them honestly,
speaking to their needs rather than fitting them into a slot in
a questionnaire.

As I read the New Testament, I am constantly struck
by the caution with which knowledge is touched upon.
Usually, when it is wholeheartedly commended, it is "the
knowledge of Christ." But knowledge *as such* is often hedged
about with cautionary words. Why? Can it be such a dangerous thing? How can knowing the truth, which must be
God's truth whatever area it lies in, be a bad thing?

It seems to me that the danger lies not in knowledge
itself, but in us — in our ineradicable tendency to use knowledge wrongly. Sin has nothing to work on, really, but that.
Only God can create, and what He creates is good. The
evil comes in taking the good God has made in wrong ways,

at wrong times, or using it for wrong purposes. The story of Adam and Eve is centered about this — the fruit of the knowledge of good and evil, which sounds so beneficial, turns out to be purely destructive. The pair had hardly eaten the fruit when their former innocence was smothered by anxiety and furtiveness and guilt. Knowledge, which in itself is such a good thing, becomes in our hands an instrument of pride.

We can see this in children all the time. In them the emotions which are cleverly camouflaged in adults are nakedly exposed for all to see. Hardly does a child acquire some new information, which might give him the means of helping his fellows, when he is hitting them over the head with it: "I know something you don't know! I'm smarter than you are!" And that is basically the story of mankind's use of knowledge — *I'm smarter than you are*. I'll use my knowledge to get the better of you, to keep you in your place, to be sure I'm better off than you are.

For this reason Christians are cautioned to be careful in their use of knowledge. We must have it, but it will always be a double-edged tool, to be handled with respect. That is why we keep coming across cautionary warnings about its use, often coupled with admonitions to let knowledge be wrapped in love.

We Do Not Know . . .

The reminder that we are "looking at puzzling reflections in a mirror," knowing only "a little fraction of the truth" is necessary because, knowing a little of God's love and His plan for mankind, we easily imagine we know it all. Besides making us foolishly proud, this attitude makes us insensitive to others — and boring as well. People who know everything (they keep telling us) are hopelessly dull. One of the saddest things about the earnest efforts at "witnessing" made by many Christians is that they are merely tedious. No one is interested. To a man just becoming aware of the depths of mystery in the universe and beginning his first groping gestures toward God, having it all explained to him by a zealous Christian (who has absorbed a book on soul-winning cover to cover) is like having his first love dissected in terms of biological urges. We might well take to heart the words of Paul, "It is easy to think that we 'know' over problems like this, but we should remember that while knowledge may make a man look big, it is only love that can make him grow to his full stature" (I Corinthians 8:1).

Those of us who have no hesitation in laying out God's timetable might well recollect also Paul's remark that we do not know how to pray worthily as sons of God, but that His Spirit within us is praying for us. If we cannot even pray rightly, we certainly are in no position to explain the whole purpose of God's work in the world, complete with charts and graphs.

This is not to say we don't know enough to carry on as God's children. He has told us all we need to know to follow Him, but He has not given us the blueprints of His dealings with men. The obvious fact that stares us in the face is that people are never won to Christ by having enough information about Him. They are drawn by His love. We are here to convey that love to them, and what a pity it is that we are constantly trying to side-step the heart of the matter by arguing them into meeting Him.

It might be good for us to remind ourselves daily that there is quite a lot God has not told us — and so we cannot tell the world. We have guidelines in the Bible, but we have no right to make rigid rules where the Bible merely indicates or suggests or hints. I know that this statement will elicit protests from many Christians who think it heresy to even whisper that there are areas of life outside our sphere of knowledge. But that reaction is simply an indication of our inherent sinfulness. If I were to say, "We do not love enough," everyone would merely sigh and agree. But to say we don't know everything arouses fierce anger, which is often an indication of inner uncertainty.

Once a number of us from various denominations were discussing baptism. Suddenly one of the men jumped up, exclaimed, "I won't even sit in this room and discuss this!" and flung himself out. We weren't quarrelling, nor was the discussion even heated — it was just that baptism was one subject upon which he could not bear to touch. His mind was made up, and he would not hear any further talk of it. It was inevitable for the rest of us to conclude that he was inwardly very uncertain, and so any discussion was a threat to him.

It's very interesting, in reading the New Testament, to notice that while there is no doubt at all about the real issues of life — faith in Christ, love for the brethren, honesty, forbearance, generosity, and so forth — there the certainty ends. We find no discussion of some of the specific actions we would have liked a pronouncement on — what we might term "worldly practices," the "do's" and the "don'ts." Even on witnessing we are given little direct instruction, only told in passing to speak pleasantly but never sentimentally, and to learn how to give a proper answer to every questioner.

But there is a great deal said about living together in love, being kind and patient with each other, doing our work well, conducting our affairs in honesty — all matters which we have been given plenty of instruction about. No lack of knowledge there — only lack of will. Really, it isn't the things we don't know about God's will that are going to hurt us, it's the things we do know and don't do.

We Know God's Love

There is in each of us a longing, however dimly felt, to penetrate the secrets of the world in which we live. We could hardly help but feel that way. We are creatures who have lost our place of command in the universe and now must exist in it as aliens. But we do have something to look forward to: "the time will come when I shall know it as fully as God now knows me!"

The thing to remember is that we have been given a kind of knowledge the rest of the world doesn't have, a knowledge of God's love for us. We have also been given the new life to live that love, to be, in reality, His ambassadors. We haven't been told all His secrets; We cannot make His appointments for Him; but we can introduce Him to others. No one is looking for a new and better explanation of life's puzzles. They are looking for evidence of lives in touch with the God who will unravel the puzzles. We don't have to give answers, we have to give evidence — and that is what witnessing really is. It ought to be encouraging to us to read that "we are men looking at puzzling reflections in a mirror but the time will come when I shall know." Because the one thing we can do, limited but not hampered by lack of knowledge, is to love.

Never fear, when we are living in love we won't be boring, as those who reduce everything to statistics are; or arrogant, as those who know it all. But we will be winning, for Christ's sake — not arguments but men.

12. WE DO
WHAT
WE ARE

In this life we have three great lasting qualities — faith, hope and love. But the greatest of them is love.
— I Corinthians 13:13

Recently, two new books were given to me by a friend. Both were written about specific techniques of successful living; one is filled with the language of the New Testament, the other with the language of psychology. Both stressed the vital importance of love — being able to love and willing to receive love. These two books are additions to the hundreds of others already written to advocate a special technique or key to successful, happy, productive and helpful living. Some are Christian, some are not; many have been of immense benefit to those who have taken them seriously. This book is not an attempt to supersede the many fine ones directed toward those who want their lives to be more meaningful than they now are. Nor is it an effort to "say the last word." No one can do that.

The very fact that there are so many "how-to" or "the secret of" books written, however, testifies to the fact that what works for one person does nothing for his neighbor, although both may try to use the same technique. Furthermore, while the techniques vary, each book claims to have an answer to life's problems which always works, when properly used. I submit that the root of the matter lies not in the specific technique, for all these techniques have proven helpful to some and not to others, but in what lies beneath the technique or method — acceptance of help from outside ourselves.

The Initiative of Love

For the Christian, the ultimate question of life is not, "How successful are you?" It is not even, "How loving are you?" or "How well are you fulfilling your potential as a child of God?" The ultimate question is, "Do you belong to Christ?" If the answer is, "Yes," then one can proceed about the business of living out the life of Christ with all the fervor and intelligence one has — using all the help one can get. The predominant flavor of the New Testament is love, and John reminds us that "love comes from God." Again and again, in every book of the New Testament, we see that it is possible for us to love only because God loves us and has given us the ability to love.

In some this ability is warped and weakened by misfortunes of heredity and environment. In others it is shriveled by the sins of temperament, or frozen by pride and arrogance. In none of us is it perfectly developed. The one great fact that we never get beyond, or cease to need, is the constant reminder that it is God who works within us, not we ourselves. The good we do, the love we show, are all received, not inherent. We never get past the point of receiving God's love; we live on it every day, as the ancient

Jews in the wilderness lived on the manna every day and could not store it up.

The great spiritual qualities of life — faith, hope and love — are all derived qualities. God designed us so that we cannot acquire them on our own, but only in Him. As a matter of fact, once we think they are our own, they begin to spoil, and some of the caricatures of love we have dis cussed are the result. Our great safety lies in constant dependence upon Christ, a dependence which protects us from the folly of imagining ourselves to be able to function independently, to "set up on our own."

It's always easy, and dangerous, to generalize. Yet it is impossible not to observe that the qualities of life the New Testament emphasizes are available to anyone willing to submit himself to the reign of Christ in his life. These are not the things we usually are impressed by, nor are they sought after by the world. Intellectual brilliance, beauty, wit, talent, even shrewdness are looked up to and envied by those who do not have them. A man or woman with one or more of these at his command can indeed feel himself superior, can say he has no need of God. True, these are all good things and many Christians possess them; but they are not spiritual. They are enjoyed indiscriminately by Christians and non-Christians alike. Their presence in a life says nothing about whether the man is good or bad. Nor do they incline either toward goodness or badness. They are like the color of one's hair or eyes, or the pigment of one's skin, or the social standing of one's ancestors; nice to have, perhaps, but making no difference in the direction of life. In a sense, they are accidents of birth.

The Bible is not concerned with these things, for they all end with death. Its concern is with the essential person — brilliant or slow, volatile or phlegmatic, gifted or ordinary — each a unique soul destined for eternity. Whether it is eternal felicity or a never-ending sojourn in the hell of separation from God depends not on one's abilities, but on the spiritual set of life. And this "set" or direction comes not with the accidents of birth but from a living commitment to Christ.

That is why we read much about faith and trust and righteousness and love, and all the qualities wrapped up in them, but very little about excellence in intellect or ability. Furthermore, the Christian virtues do not commonly excite envy. Wonder, perhaps, or amazement that they could exist in such a world, but not envy. Oh, we sometimes hear carping comments about so-and-so's many friends; "I'd like to know what they see in him. He's not so much." But these are usually the reaction of the bitter, lonely people toward those who are loved because they are loving. The envy is simply directed toward the rewards of virtue, not toward the virtue itself.

One of the commonest mistakes we all make is to assume that people will love us because there is something admirable or unusual or superior about us; hence the many pathetic attempts to impress by boasting or showing off. Think about yourself. Do you love your friends because they are so talented, so superior? I don't. I love my friends because they love me and respond to me. This works both ways, of course. When there is a spark of rapport between two people, friendship or love can begin to grow. Our relationship to God, however, is always one of response. We do not initiate, He does. In the words of John, we love Him *because* He first loved us.

The love which comes from God is *more than* any human love. All human love derives from God, the source of love. But when love in the Christian's life is transformed by Christ's life in us, it becomes more than purely human love. We begin, in a very small way, to share in the love of God as He is working it out in the world.

The Response of Love

We can see, then, how important it is that our human love be constantly infused with the life of Christ in us so that we really share in the new life of love God has planned for us. We cannot accomplish this once and then just automatically conform to it. Such infusion is a daily, even minutely (if we can express it that way) acceptance of His will in our lives. Furthermore, the love God has for us and wants to work out in us is not emotion, or feeling, although emotion may be present. It is, again, a "set of mind," a deliberate willing of the individual to do what God wants. That doing means living in harmony and in love with the Christian family. This is repeated over and over in the New Testament — *the proof of our standing with Christ is our relationship with His children.*

It would be just lovely if all Christians were automatically straightened out by Christ, so that old attitudes disappeared without our being aware of it, and we had all the right motives, all the right emotions, and lived in love just as unthinkingly as we used to live in self-centeredness. But that is not how the Christian life works. It is unrealistic to expect God to do for us the things He has told *us* to do. If no effort were involved, He wouldn't have had to tell us — and tell us so painstakingly, in so many ways.

Read Paul's writings carefully. Every letter begins with instruction in doctrine. Paul tells us what God has done, and the meaning of His acts. Following the doctrine comes practical instruction on what this means in daily life. *This* is true, therefore live this way. Certain great central themes are found in every letter, so we conclude they are very much the heart of the Gospel. All of them can be compressed into the sentence, "Thou shalt love the Lord thy God with all thy heart, and with all thy soul and with all thy mind, and thou shalt love thy neighbor as thyself."

Everyone knows that quotation. But because we have to unlearn, as it were, all the willful, self-centered, fearful and suspicious patterns of thinking and living we were heir to, we need to read and study the whole Bible constantly. That is how we find out what we must do to make this new love in our lives work out in practical living. Sometimes it's easy, more often it is not. Situations and temperaments do not commonly bend themselves to adjust to our needs. So we are constantly being faced with problems and personalities which elicit from us not love but irritation or even hatred.

On the human level we would respond, when met with a rebuff, with anger. That is just natural, animal reaction. The new dimension in which we move, however, as children of God, loved by Him, redeemed by Christ, really lifts us out of that old level of cause and effect. In these situations we can begin to act, not in reaction to the situation but in response to God's love. Admittedly such action doesn't come easily or without effort — but we are told to ask of God when we have needs, and He helps us. We will fail at times; we will love imperfectly often; we will never arrive at the place where we do not need to turn constantly to Christ for His strength and love. But we will be becoming, slowly and painfully, what God intends for us to be. And, though we may not see it at the time, in this process we are helping one another.

In looking back over my own life it is clear that I am where I am now because of what my Christian friends and family have done for me. In a sense, they rubbed off on me. Or you might say I "caught" the love of Christ they were living much as I caught the measles. The Christian life, C. S. Lewis said, is "good infection." And there is nothing so highly contagious as the love of God being lived out in a human life.

We Do What We Are

There has always been, in the Christian view of man, a puzzling dichotomy. Sometimes the Bible speaks of the "heart" or the will of man as being the determining factor in his destiny. At other times it talks as if how a man behaves is the only criterion by which God judges him. This is not a dichotomy between the Old Testament and the New, for both viewpoints are found in both places.

The resolving of this apparent problem lies in the words of Jesus.

> "A good man produces good things from the good stored up in his heart, and a bad man produces evil things from his own stores of evil. For a man's words will always express what has been treasured in his heart."

And not a man's words only, but his deeds show what he is, for the Lord continued His discourse by saying, "And what is the point of calling me, 'Lord, Lord,' without doing what I tell you to do?" (Luke 6:40,46).

The Bible is really speaking with a deeper consistency than appears on the surface when it speaks both of one's inner set of mind and one's deeds as being determinative of what we really are. *We do what we are.* True, all of us fail miserably at times, and even the worst of men occasionally show some evidence of human affection. So it is never possible to judge another man's standing by an isolated deed. But in the main, the tenor of our lives reveals what we are.

However, we are told so many times in the Bible not to judge one another that we ought to pay attention to the warning. Much safer to look to ourselves to see whether or not *we* are conforming to the mind of Christ than to examine others. The world judges us — that is very evident — and we are responsible before God for our conduct in the world. Peter tells us: "Your conduct among the surrounding peoples in your different countries should always be good and right, so that although they may in the usual way slander you as evildoers, yet when disasters come they may glorify God when they see how well you conduct yourselves" (I Peter 2:12).

The love that the Bible describes in action produces good attitudes and deeds out of an inner quality of love which we do not have on our own but which comes from God. Our natural affections, changeable and intermittent as they can be, are not enough; they need to be transformed by Christ's love, and that is what happens in the Christian life.

We never get to the place of perfection. But we are heading in the right direction, and the visible evidence of that direction is the kind of life we live. There is surely something seriously wrong with someone who claims to know Christ and yet who never exhibits anything of His love and compassion. Therefore we must examine ourselves, not for our spirituality, for that kind of introspection leads either to pride or despair, but for our faithfulness to Christ's commands. The question is not, "How am I being treated?" but, "How am I treating others?"

A genuine concern for others might well replace our neurotic absorption in our own spirituality. Not "How well am I witnessing?" but "What am I witnessing?" One can "witness" in the obvious sense of giving a testimony, without love — but love is its own witness, a never-failing evidence of Christ in our lives.

"Let Us Love . . ."

In the end most of us will say, "We did not love enough," and it will be true. I felt, as everyone has felt after the death of someone we love, that I had not been loving enough to my husband. I didn't wish I had been more intelligent about his business, or more busy with the housework, or more entertaining in my conversation, or any of the trivial things we often concern ourselves with. I wished I had been more loving. This is what we all find ourselves confessing — our best is not good enough.

My comfort and my hope for the future lie in the forgiveness and renewal I find in Christ. It is humiliating but somehow very bracing to face God in prayer, confessing my lack of love, and accepting His cleansing and forgiving and accepting love. I can go on. So can we all, not with any expectation of arriving, some day, at a point of perfection, but with the assurance that our sins are forgiven — first among them our lack of love — and that we are, in daily commitment to Christ, becoming what He has declared us to be.

One last thing. When we have done all we can, spoken and acted the best that we could, there comes a time when one can do no more — except for one thing. We can love. Imperfectly, sometimes stumblingly, we can go on giving ourselves to Christ so that He can give Himself more completely to us. Our love loses its limitedness in His limitless love.

GLOSSARY OF LOVE

The Lord did not set his love upon you, nor choose you, because you were more in number than any people; for ye were the fewest of all people: but because the Lord loved you, and because he would keep the oath which he had sworn unto your fathers, hath the Lord brought you out with a mighty hand, and redeemed you out of the house of bondmen, from the hand of Pharaoh king of Egypt. — Deut. 7:7-8

Hatred stirreth up strifes: but love covereth all sins. — Prov. 10: 12

A friend loveth at all times, and a brother is born for adversity. — Prov. 17:17

Set me as a seal upon thine heart, as a seal upon thine arm: for love is as strong as death; jealousy is as cruel as the grave. . . . Many waters cannot quench love, neither can the floods drown it: if a man would give all the substance of his house for love, it would be utterly contemned. — Song of Sol. 8:6, 7

The Lord hath appeared of old unto me, saying, Yea, I have loved thee with an everlasting love: therefore with lovingkindness have I drawn thee. — Jer. 31:3

"You have heard that it used to be said 'Thou shalt love thy neighbor and hate thine enemy,' but I tell you, Love your enemies, and pray for those who persecute you, so that you may be sons of your Heavenly Father. For he makes his sun rise upon evil men as well as good, and he sends his rain upon honest and dishonest men alike.

"For if you love only those who love you, what credit is that to you? Even tax-collectors do that! . . . No, you are to be perfect, like your Heavenly Father." — Matt. 5: 43-48

"It was because you knew so little of the meaning of love that Moses allowed you to divorce your wives! But that was not the original principle. I tell you that anyone who divorces his wife on any grounds except her unfaithfulness, and marries some other woman, commits adultery." — Matt. 19:8, 9

" 'Thou shalt love the Lord thy God with all thy heart, and with all thy soul and with all thy mind.' This is the first and great commandment. And there is a second like it: 'Thou shalt love thy neighbor as thyself.' The whole of the Law and the Prophets depends on these two commandments." — Matt. 22:37-40

"But I say to all of you who will listen to me: love your enemies, do good to those who hate you, bless those who curse you, and pray for those who treat you badly." — Luke 6:27, 28

". . . her sins, many as they are, are forgiven; for she has shown me so much love. But the man who has little to be forgiven has only a little love to give." — Luke 7:47

Then one of the experts in the Law stood up to test him and said, "Master, what must I do to be sure of eternal life?"

"What does the Law say . . .?" said Jesus.

"The Law says, 'Thou shalt love the Lord thy God with all thy heart and with all thy soul and with all thy strength and with all thy mind — and thy neighbor as thyself,'" he replied.

"Quite right," said Jesus. "Do that and you will live."

But the man, wanting to justify himself, continued,

"But who is my 'neighbor'?"

And Jesus gave him the following reply:

"A man was once on his way down from Jerusalem to Jericho. He fell into the hands of bandits who stripped off his clothes, beat him up, and left him half dead. It so happened that a priest . . . passed by on the other side. A Levite also . . . passed by on the other side. But then a Samaritan traveler came along . . . and at the sight of him was touched with pity. He . . . bandaged his wounds . . . brought him to an inn and . . . took out two silver coins, and gave them to the innkeeper. . . . Which of these three seems to you to have been a neighbor to the bandits' victim?"

"The man who gave him practical sympathy," he replied.

"Then you go and give the same," returned Jesus. — Luke 10: 25-37

"Now I am giving you a new command — love one another. Just as I have loved you, you must love one another. This is how all men will know that you are my disciples, because you have such love for one another." — John 13:34, 35

"If you really love me, you will keep the commandments I have given you and I shall ask the Father to give you someone else to stand by you, to be with you always. . . .

"Every man who knows my commandments and obeys them is the man who really loves me. . . ." — John 14:15, 16, 21

"I have loved you just as the Father has loved me. You must go on living in my love. If you keep my commandments you will live in my love just as I have kept my Father's commandments and live in his love. I have told you this so that you can share my joy, and that your happiness may be complete. This is my commandment: that you love one another as I have loved you. There is no greater love than this — that a man should lay down his life for his friends. You are my friends if you do what I tell you to do." — John 15:9-14

. . . Jesus said to Simon Peter, "Simon, son of John, do you love me more than these others?"

"Yes, Lord," he replied, "you know that I am your friend."

"Then feed my lambs," returned Jesus. Then he said for the second time,

"Simon, son of John, do you love me?"

"Yes, Lord," returned Peter. "You know that I am your friend."

"Then care for my sheep," replied Jesus. — John 21:15, 16

Yet the proof of God's amazing love is this: that it was *while we were sinners* that Christ died for us. — Rom. 5:8

Moreover we know that to those who love God, who are called according to his plan, everything that happens fits into a pattern for good. . . .

Who can separate us from the love of Christ? Can trouble, pain or persecution? Can lack of clothes and food, danger to life and limb, the threat of force of arms? . . .

No, in all these things we win an overwhelming victory through him who has proved his love for us.

I have become absolutely convinced that neither death nor life, neither messenger of Heaven nor monarch of earth, neither what happens today nor what may happen tomorrow, neither a power from on high nor a power from below, nor anything else in God's whole world has any power to separate us from the love of God in Christ Jesus our Lord! — Rom. 8:28, 35-39

Let us have no imitation Christian love. Let us have a genuine break with evil and a real devotion to good. Let us have real warm affection for one another as between brothers, and a willingness to let the other man have the credit. — Rom. 12:9, 10

Keep out of debt altogether, except that perpetual debt of love which we owe one another. The man who loves his neighbor has obeyed the whole Law in regard to his neighbor. For the commandments, "Thou shalt not commit adultery," "Thou shalt not kill," "Thou shalt not steal," "Thou shalt not covet" and all other commandments are summed up in this one saying: "Thou shalt love thy neighbor as thyself." Love hurts nobody: therefore love is the answer to the Law's commands. — Rom. 13:8-10

. . . we should remember that while knowledge may make a man look big, it is only love that can make him grow to his full stature. For whatever a man may know, he still has a lot to learn; but if he loves God, he is opening his whole life to the Spirit of God. — I Cor. 8:1-3

There was a reason for my stern words; this is my advice now. If the behaviour of a certain person has caused distress, it does not mean so much that he has injured me, but that to some extent . . . he has injured all of you. But now I think that the punishment you have inflicted on him has been sufficient. Now is the time to offer forgiveness and comfort, for it is possible for a man in his position to be completely overwhelmed by remorse. I ask you to show him plainly now that you love him. — II Cor. 2:5-8

The very spring of our actions is the love of Christ. — II Cor. 5:14

Children don't have to put by their savings for their parents; parents do that for their children. Consequently I will most gladly spend and be spent for your good, even though it means that the more I love you the less you love me. — II Cor. 12:14, 15

The bodily life I now live, I live believing in the Son of God, who loved me and sacrificed himself for me. Consequently I refuse to stultify the grace of God by reverting to the Law. — Gal. 2:20, 21

The Spirit, however, produces in human life fruits such as these: love, joy, peace, patience, kindness, generosity, fidelity, tolerance and self-control — and no law exists against any of them.

Those who belong to Christ Jesus have crucified their old nature with all that it loved and lusted for. — Gal. 5:22-24

He planned, in his purpose of love, that we should be adopted as his own children through Jesus Christ — that we might learn to praise that glorious generosity of his which has made us welcome in the everlasting love he bears towards the Beloved. — Eph. 1:5-7

But even though we were dead in our sins God, who is rich in mercy, because of the great love he had for us, gave us life together with Christ — it is, remember, by grace and not by achievement that you are saved — and has lifted us right out of the old life to take our place with him in Christ Jesus in the Heavens. . . . No one can pride himself upon earning the love of God. — Eph. 2:4-6, 9

And I pray that you, firmly fixed in love yourselves, may be able to grasp (with all Christians) how wide and deep and long and high is the love of Christ — and to know for yourselves that love so far beyond our comprehension. May you be filled through all your being with God himself! — Eph. 3: 17-19

Accept life with humility and patience, making allowances for one another because you love one another. — Eph. 4:2

We are not meant to remain as children at the mercy of every chance wind of teaching and the jockeying of men who are expert in the crafty presentation of lies. But we are meant to hold firmly to the truth in love, and to grow up in every way into Christ, the head. — Eph. 4:14, 15

As children copy their fathers you, as God's children, are to copy him. Live your lives in love — the same sort of love which Christ gives us and which he perfectly expressed when he gave himself up for us in sacrifice to God. — Eph. 5:1, 2

But, remember, this means that the husband must give his wife the same sort of love that Christ gave to the Church, when he sacrificed himself for her. — Eph. 5:25

My prayer for you is that you may have still more love — a love that is full of knowledge and wise insight. — Phil. 1:9

Now if your experience of Christ's encouragement and love means anything to you, if you have known something of the fellowship of His Spirit and all that it means in kindness and deep sympathy, do make my best hopes for you come true! Live together in harmony, live together in love, as though you had only one mind and one spirit between you. Never act from motives of rivalry or personal vanity, but in humility think more of each other than you do of yourselves. None of you should think only of his own affairs, but should learn to see things from other people's point of view. — Phil. 2:1-4

I want you to know by this letter that we here are constantly praying for you, and whenever we do we thank God the Father of our Lord Jesus Christ because you believe in Christ Jesus and because you are showing true Christian love towards other Christians. We know that you are showing these qualities because you have grasped the hope reserved for you in Heaven — that hope, which first became yours when the truth was brought to you. — Col. 1:3-6

How I long that you may be encouraged, and find out more and more how strong are the bonds of Christian love. — Col. 2:2

As, therefore, God's picked representatives of the new humanity, purified and beloved of God himself, be merciful in action, kindly in heart, humble in mind. Accept life, and be most patient and tolerant with one another, always ready to forgive if you have a difference with anyone. Forgive as freely as the Lord has forgiven you. And, above everything else, be truly loving, for love is the golden chain of all the virtues. — Col. 3:12-14

Wives, adapt yourselves to your husbands, that your marriage may be a Christian unity. Husbands, be sure you give your wives much love and sympathy; don't let bitterness or resentment spoil your marriage. As for you children, your duty is to obey your parents, for at your age this is one of the best things you can do to show your love for the Lord. — Col. 3: 18-20

Because we loved you, it was a joy to us to give you not only the gospel of God but our very hearts — so dear did you become to us. — I Thess. 2:8

May the Lord give you the same increasing and overflowing love for one another and toward all men as we have toward you. — I Thess. 3:12

Next, as regards brotherly love, you don't need any written instructions. God himself is teaching you to love one another, and you are already extending your love to all the Macedonians. Yet we urge you to have more and more of this love, and to make it your ambition to have no ambition! — I Thess. 4:9-11

But we can thank God continually for you, brothers, whom the Lord loves. He has chosen you from the beginning to save you, to make you holy by the work of his Spirit and your own belief in the truth. — II Thess. 2:13

The ultimate aim of the Christian ministry, after all, is to produce the love which springs from a pure heart, a good conscience and a genuine faith. — I Tim. 1:5

Our Lord poured out his grace upon me, giving me tremendous faith in, and love for, himself. — I Tim. 1:14

For God has not given us a spirit of fear, but a spirit of power and love and a sound mind. — II Tim. 1:7

Turn your back on the turbulent desires of youth and give your positive attention to goodness, faith, love and peace in company with all those who approach God in sincerity. — II Tim. 2:22

But you Timothy . . . saw my endurance and love and patience as I met all those persecutions and difficulties at Antioch, Iconium and Lystra. — II Tim. 3:10, 11

Never let your brotherly love fail, nor refuse to extend your hospitality to strangers — sometimes men have entertained angels unawares. — Heb. 13:1, 2

If you obey the royal law, expressed by the scripture, "Thou shalt love thy neighbor as thyself," all is well. But once you allow any invidious distinctions to creep in, you are sinning; you have broken God's Law. — James 2:8, 9

Now that you have, by obeying the truth, made your souls clean enough for a genuine love of your fellows, see that you do love one another, fervently and from the heart. — I Peter 1:22

To sum up, you should all be of one mind living like brothers with true love and sympathy for one another, generous and courteous at all times. Never pay back a bad turn with a bad turn or an insult with another insult, but on the contrary pay back with good. — I Pet. 3:8, 9

Above everything else be sure that you have real deep love for one another, remembering how love can "cover a multitude of sins." Be hospitable to one another without secretly wishing you hadn't got to be! Serve one another with the particular gifts God has given each of you, as faithful dispensers of the magnificently varied grace of God. — I Pet. 4:8-10

Your goodness must be accompanied by knowledge, your knowledge by self-control, your self-control by the ability to endure. Your endurance too must always be accompanied by devotion to God; that in turn must have in it the quality of brotherliness, and your brotherliness must lead on to Christian love. — II Pet. 1:1-7

It is only when we obey God's laws that we can be quite sure that we really know him. The man who claims to know God but does not obey his laws is not only a liar but lives in self-delusion. In practice, the more a man learns to obey God's laws, the more truly and fully does he express his love for him. Obedience is the test of whether we really live "in God" or not. The life of a man who professes to be living in God must bear the stamp of Christ. — I John 2:3-6

We know that we have crossed the frontier from death to life because we do love our brothers. The man without love for his brother is living in death already. The man who actively hates his brother is a potential murderer, and you will readily see that the eternal life of God cannot live in the heart of a murderer.

We know and to some extent realize the love of God for us be-cause Christ expressed it in laying down his life for us. We must in turn express our love by laying down our lives for those who are our brothers. But as for the well-to-do man who sees his brother in want but shuts his eyes — and his heart — how could anyone believe that the love of God lives in him? My children, let us love not merely in theory or in words — let us love in sincerity and practice! — I John 3:14-18

To you whom I love I say, let us go on loving one another, for love comes from God. Every man who truly loves is God's son and has some knowledge of him. But the man who does not love cannot know him at all, for God is love.

To us, the greatest demonstration of God's love for us has been his sending his only Son into the world to give us life through him. We see real love, not in the fact that we loved God, but that he loved us and sent his Son to make personal atonement for our sins. If God loved us as much as that, surely we, in our turn, should love one another! . . . if we love one another God does actually live within us, and his love grows in us towards perfection. . . . Love contains no fear — indeed fully developed love expels every particle of fear, for fear always contains some of the torture of feeling guilty. — I John 4:11, 12, 18

For God loved the world so much that he gave his only Son so that everyone who believes in him should not be lost, but should have eternal life. — John 3:16